Contents

KU-506-970

1 The survey

1.1 Samples and censuses

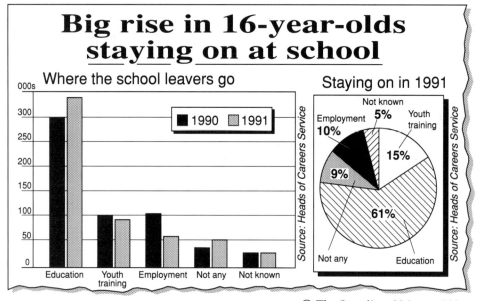

Big rise in 16-year-olds staying on at school

Where the school leavers go

Staying on in 1991

Source: Heads of Careers Service

© *The Guardian*: 23 June 1992

Many newspaper articles and headlines are based upon statistical data. A variety of diagrams is used to make these data easy to understand.

About 100 000 16-year-olds left school for youth training in 1990.

(a) Use the histogram to estimate the total number of 16-year-olds staying on in education in 1990.

(b) Estimate the number of 16-year-olds in the other categories.

(c) Use your answers to (a) and (b) to estimate how many 16-year-olds there were in total in 1990.

(d) Calculate percentages and draw a pie chart for 1990, similar to the one shown for 1991.

(e) Is the conclusion of the newspaper headline justified?

Handling data

The School Mathematics Project

CAMBRIDGE
UNIVERSITY PRESS

Main authors   Rob Coe
                       Paul Roder
                       Jeff Searle

Team leader   Paul Roder

The authors and publisher are grateful to:

The Guardian for permission to reproduce the extract on page 4;
The Open University for permission to reproduce the diagram on page 5;
HMSO/Central Statistical Office for permission to reproduce the extract on page 32;
The Economist Books for permission to reproduce the extracts on pages 34 and 46.

The authors and publisher would like to thank the following for supplying photographs:

front cover – Runners, The Telegraph Colour Library;
page 22 – Alan Edwards.

Cartoons by Gordon Hendry

Published by the Press Syndicate of the University of Cambridge
The Pitt Building, Trumpington Street, Cambridge CB2 1RP
40 West 20th Street, New York, NY 10011–4211, USA
10 Stamford Road, Oakleigh, Melbourne 3166, Australia

First published 1993
Reprinted 1994

Produced by Gecko Limited, Bicester, Oxon

Cover design by Iguana Creative Design

Printed in Great Britain at the University Press, Cambridge

A catalogue record for this book is available from the British Library

Library of Congress cataloguing in publication data applied for

ISBN 0 521 447321 paperback

Notice to teachers

Suppose you decided to carry out a similar survey for last year's
16-year-olds at your own school or college. The set of all these
students forms the **population** in which you are interested. You
could try to find out the destination of all of last year's 16-year-olds.
A survey based on an entire population is called a **census**.

To carry out a census for your school might be difficult, especially if
there is a large number of students. Most surveys are based on a
sample picked at random from the population.

For your school or college:

(a) If you decide to use a sample, who would you ask?

(b) What questions would you ask?

(c) How would you set about collecting the data?

A statistical investigation goes through four distinct stages:

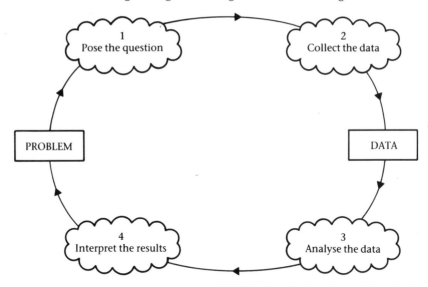

Statistical investigations in secondary schools

This chapter will look at the first two stages: posing the question and
collecting the data. Although the rest of the book is mainly
concerned with the analysis and interpretation of data, the first two
stages are important because:

● if you do not ask sensible questions then your data will not be
  suitable for analysing;

● the interpretation will be meaningless if you have not selected a
  sample which genuinely represents the population from which it
  is selected.

5

1.2 Pose the question

The most difficult part of a survey is posing the question. You must have a very clear idea of what you want to find out. Remember, the quality of your data and the subsequent analysis of those data depend on your asking the right questions.

Here are some guidelines for asking questions. Questions must:

- be **clear**. A question such as 'How much television do you watch?' is unclear. Do you mean how many hours per day? – or per week? Responses such as 'Not a lot' or 'About average' would be difficult to analyse.

- be **neutral**. A leading question is one which appears to expect a certain answer. For example the question 'Do you agree that there is too much football on TV?' is a leading question as it seems to expect the answer 'Yes'.

- be **reasonable**. A person should be able to answer a question quickly. It is unreasonable to expect people to spend time writing long sentences, looking up information, etc. in response to a question. Unless a questionnaire is easy to answer it will have a poor response rate. (People will not bother to answer it.)

- **not give offence**. Even questions which may appear innocent can give offence. For example, many people may not want to reveal their age, waist measurement or social background.

One way of avoiding many potential problems is to have 'Yes/No' answers, or to ask people to tick a box.

For example, the following questions can be answered quickly.

National Survey

Are you a regular church-goer?   Yes [ ]   No [ ]

Are you in favour of Sunday trading?

Yes [ ]   No [ ]   Undecided [ ]

However, even questions which look straightforward can cause problems. For example, someone may want to know if a synagogue or a mosque counts as a church. A person may be against Sunday trading but want to be able to buy a Sunday paper.

Problems of interpretation can often be overcome when an interviewer asks the questions and fills in the questionnaire. Any problems can then be sorted out on the spot.

As mentioned earlier, it is most important to be very clear about what it is you want to find out. You should not ask unnecessary questions and must try to keep the questionnaire brief.

Criticise the following questions and in each case suggest a way of improving them.

(a) How big are you?

(b) What do you think of the present government?

(c) How much do you spend on clothes?   Less than average [ ]
About average [ ]
More than average [ ]

(d) What do you think of the new improved canteen menu?

After you have compiled your questionnaire, try it out on a few people to see if it works. This form of trial run is called a **pilot survey** and is a good way of improving your questionnaire. You will usually discover poor questions fairly quickly.

1.3 Collect the data

Having decided what questions you want to ask, you now need to decide on your sample. If, for instance, you are going to ask people to fill in a questionnaire, the people you ask (the sample) should be representative. Ideally, their responses should reflect those of the whole population.

If you want to sample the views of students at your school or college it is probably not a good idea to ask twenty of your friends and no one else. Your friends may share your views on many issues, and these views may not be those of most students.

A sample is like a window through which you can see a small part of a population.

If it is representative, a sample will give reliable information about the population, that is if there is no **bias** in the way the sample is selected.

There is a famous example of an opinion poll giving the wrong result because of bias, when in 1948 a major telephone poll predicted victory for Dewey, the Republican candidate in the US presidential election. In the event, Truman, the Democrat candidate, won the election. The incorrect forecast was due to bias in the way the sample was selected. People who owned telephones were not representative of the voting population since at that time only the higher-paid voters owned telephones.

Why might there be bias in the method for picking the sample in each of the following?

(a) A secondary school is holding its own mock election just before a general election. A pupil asks the other pupils in the class how they intend to vote. This is then used to predict the result for the school.

(b) A student is doing a survey into students' attitudes to the college canteen. She picks students at random from the dinner queue as her sample.

The following tasksheet will give you the opportunity to explore the scope of a statistical investigation and ask you to plan an investigation of your own, paying particular attention to how you are going to avoid bias in the selection of your sample.

 TASKSHEET 1 — Planning the survey (page 10)

You should not carry out your survey until **after** completing this book, as the rest of the book is concerned with the analysis and interpretation of statistics.

As you work through the book, consider the investigation you planned and decide where you can use the techniques you learn. Perhaps you can think of ways to adjust your questions to make better use of the techniques. You may even change your mind about the subject of your survey!

Once the plan of your investigation is complete and you have collected the data, it is a good idea to enter the data onto a **computer database**. A database can take much of the tedium out of the analysis and will even produce many of the diagrams you will need to illustrate your report. The most important part of the investigation, however, is the interpretation of your results. No database can do this for you and no investigation is complete without a conclusion.

After working through this chapter you should:

1 know the four stages of a statistical investigation;

2 understand the importance of questionnaire design;

3 understand the importance of avoiding bias in your sample;

4 know how to plan a statistical investigation.

Planning the survey

Some ideas for subjects for statistical investigations are given on this tasksheet. You can choose one of them or think of something for yourself.

When you have chosen an investigation, you must **plan** it. (Do **not** carry out the survey yet.) You must:

- state clearly what the investigation is about and why you want to explore this particular topic;

- identify clearly the population you are surveying;

- state how you intend to pick a representative sample from this population and how big your sample will be;

- explain why you think your method of sampling will avoid bias;

- show how you intend to collect your data (i.e. design a questionnaire to be filled in by the people in your sample, **or** design a set of questions plus record sheet to be filled in by an interviewer).

Ideas for investigation

- Alcohol/cigarettes: How many people drink or smoke? How much? How often?

- Part-time jobs: How many people have them? How many hours do they work? What are the rates of pay?

- Television: Who watches what? How much? How often?

- Sport: How many people are involved (spectators and participants)? Are there any trends in attendance?

- Cars: What would a survey of age, colour, make and so on show?

- Spending: How much do people spend on different items?

- Newspapers/magazines: Who reads them?

Do not be limited by these suggestions – only use them if you cannot think of any ideas of your own. It is much better to do something you are interested in.

2 Displaying frequency

2.1 Grouped data

When you have collected the data you need for your investigation, you will have to think about how they can be represented in graphs and diagrams. This chapter shows some of the techniques you can use.

The manager of a fast food restaurant wants to improve the quality of customer service and increase the restaurant's efficiency. She commissions a firm of market researchers to find out how well the restaurant is doing and how it might improve.

The researchers' task is not only to decide what data to collect, but also how to present them to the manager. Part of the information they collect concerns the amounts spent (in pence) by 30 customers in the restaurant.

270	130	266	153	398	99	289	80	457	169
112	237	80	155	345	238	189	86	279	40
153	169	334	112	487	130	370	155	237	86

It is very difficult to get an impression of the results from looking at the raw data. They need to be presented in some kind of chart or table. Tasksheet 1 compares different ways of doing this.

TASKSHEET 1 – Grouped data (page 21)

> Before data can be represented, a decision has to be made about the intervals into which they should be grouped.
>
> (a) What would be the best way to group the amounts spent? Choose several different ways and make a tally for each. (Divide this task among the class if you can.)
>
> (b) Which way is best? Why?

2.2 Frequency graphs

The market researchers could collect a large volume of data by interviewing customers in McTavish's. They need to know what kinds of graph to use for each set of data. The first thing they have to decide is whether the data are **qualitative, discrete** or **continuous**.

Qualitative data

When you ask a question where the answer is not a number (for example 'What is your favourite kind of burger?') or when you divide people into categories (for example male/female), the kind of information you obtain is qualitative. These data can be shown in bar graphs. The bars should be drawn with spaces between them.

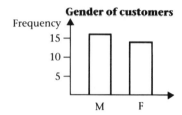

If the same information can be broken down (for example by age), you can split the bars and display them either side-by-side or end-to-end.

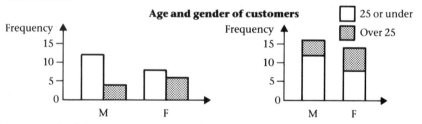

Each of the 30 people interviewed was asked to say which of the three burgers, Big McT, Quarter Pounder or McVeggie, they preferred. The results were:

	Big McT	Quarter Pounder	McVeggie
Female	3	5	6
Male	6	2	8

(a) Display these results on a bar graph.

(b) Why might McTavish's want this information?

Continuous data

If the response to a question is a **number** then the data collected will be either **discrete** or **continuous**. Continuous data consist of numbers which could take any value on a number line, with no gaps. The bars on frequency graphs for continuous data should not have gaps between them.

EXAMPLE 1

The times (in minutes and seconds) that 30 customers spent sitting down in McTavish's restaurant one Saturday morning are:

13:25	9:47	20:11	40:05	18:52	25:48
36:32	36:54	21:13	10:23	8:07	38:43
14:39	18:02	36:59	28:50	27:17	12:30
22:19	22:34	19:10	2:16	24:45	22:42
42:45	35:21	13:12	30:37	6:39	21:08

Display this information on a frequency graph.

SOLUTION

First choose suitable intervals and make a tally.

Time spent (minutes)	0–	10–	20–	30–	40–50
Tally	IIII	⌖III	⌖⌖	⌖I	II
Frequency	4	8	10	6	2

Then draw the axes of the graph so that they cover the range and frequency. The frequency graph is as shown. Note that, as time is continuous, the bars are drawn **without** gaps.

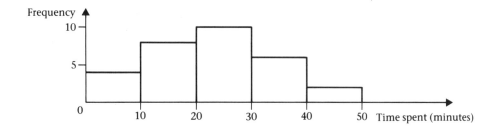

Suppose the intervals are 0–, 15– and 30–45.

(a) Produce a tally and draw the frequency graph.

(b) Do you think this choice of interval is better or worse than the one used in the example? Explain.

For continuous data:

- choose equal intervals and produce a tally;

- draw a scale that covers the range;

- plot the bars with no gaps between;

- make the height of each bar the frequency.

Discrete data

Discrete data can only take particular values. For example, the number of people sitting at a table in a group or the number of burgers sold can only take whole number values, so they are discrete. Shoe sizes are also discrete, as only certain values are possible (1, $1\frac{1}{2}$, 2, $2\frac{1}{2}$, etc.). In general, when discrete data are shown on a frequency graph the bars should be separated.

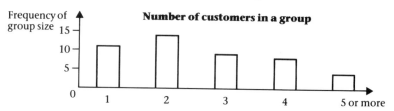

The information can also be broken down according to the time of day. For example:

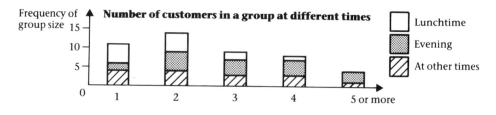

For qualitative or discrete data, frequency graphs should have gaps between the bars.

Although frequency graphs should have gaps between the bars when the data are discrete, if the data have been grouped they are sometimes displayed as though they were continuous (i.e. without gaps between the bars). On the tasksheet you saw how the amounts of money spent by 30 customers in McTavish's could be displayed on a frequency graph with gaps between the bars. This information can also be displayed on a continuous scale.

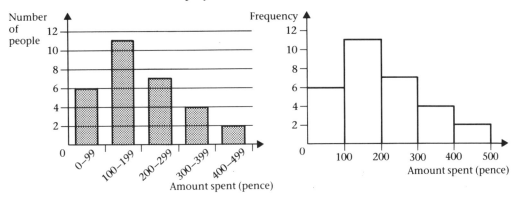

Although, in theory, there should be small gaps between 99 and 100, 199 and 200, etc. it is not practical to try to show the gaps, so the graph is drawn without them.

EXERCISE 1

1 Customers at McTavish's can either eat in the restaurant or take their food away. Twenty of the first fifty customers to visit McTavish's on a particular day took their food away while the others used the restaurant. Show this information on a frequency graph.

2 (a) Draw a graph to show the following information on the frequency of visits to McTavish's for two different age groups in a sample of 30 customers.

| | Number of visits per month | | | |
	0–4	5–9	10–14	15–19
Aged 25 or under	4	8	5	3
Aged over 25	3	5	2	0

(b) Did you draw the bars end-to-end or side-by-side? Explain how you made your choice.

(c) What is the most common number of visits per month?

(d) How would you describe the difference between the frequency of visits of the two age groups?

15

2.3 **Choosing intervals**

Whenever you draw a chart or diagram to represent information, you are bound to lose some of the detail. You have to decide what information you want the chart to show.

One of the ways you lose information is by grouping the data into intervals. For this reason the intervals you choose may be very important.

The raw data for the times 30 customers spent waiting in McTavish's can be arranged in order as shown.

0:00	0:00	0:35	1:06	1:20	1:28	1:49
2:30	2:30	2:52	3:14	3:43	4:50	5:08
5:25	5:40	6:15	6:51	7:18	8:12	8:47
10:38	11:11	11:37	13:20	14:02	16:13	16:29
17:42	19:56				(minutes:seconds)	

If you choose a large number of very small intervals, a chart will show a lot of information, but too much detail may be confusing.

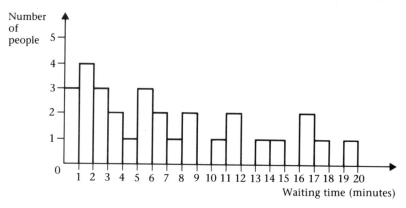

On the other hand, if you have very few intervals, the graph is simpler, but it may be too simple.

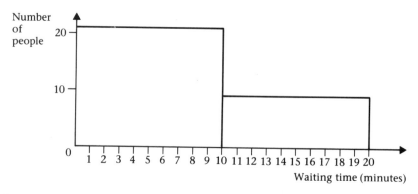

Somewhere in between the two extremes is usually best.

Neither of the previous groupings is ideal. What grouping would you recommend the market researchers to use and why?

When choosing grouped intervals:

- look at the data to find the range covered (highest and lowest values);

- decide how many intervals you need;

- divide the whole range into a number of equal intervals;

- make a tally and find the frequencies;

- if you are still satisfied with your choice, draw the chart.

EXERCISE 2

1   The amount of money (in £) taken each day by McTavish's was recorded for a fortnight as follows:

| 472 | 489 | 545 | 570 | 452 | 921 | 1097 | 506 |
| 483 | 528 | 580 | 494 | 987 | 1034 | | |

(a) Treating these as continuous data, choose suitable intervals and draw a frequency graph.

(b) How would you describe the shape of this graph? Can you explain why it is like this?

2   On a quality control test, a McThick Shake dispenser produced the following volumes of McThick Shake (in ml):

| 493 | 504 | 479 | 485 | 501 | 490 | 503 | 487 |
| 492 | 499 | 512 | 489 | 497 | 507 | 496 | 482 |

(a) Choose suitable intervals and draw a frequency graph to show this information.

(b) If a standard McThick Shake is sold as 500 ml, what changes would you make to the dispenser? Why?

2.4 Frequency polygons

One of the researchers at McTavish's collected data on how long customers had to wait before being served. She noted the waiting times for 30 customers during a Monday lunchtime and compared the data with the waiting times of 30 customers during a Saturday lunchtime.

The frequency graphs are shown below.

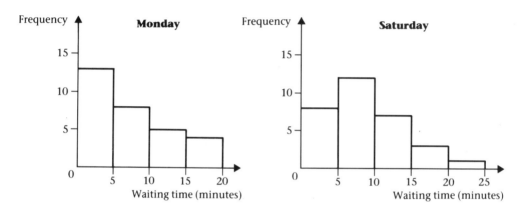

The researcher wanted to show both pieces of information on one graph to make comparisons easier. She did this by drawing **frequency polygons**. To draw a frequency polygon you simply join the mid-points of the tops of the bars with straight lines. For example, the graph for Monday's data can be drawn as shown.

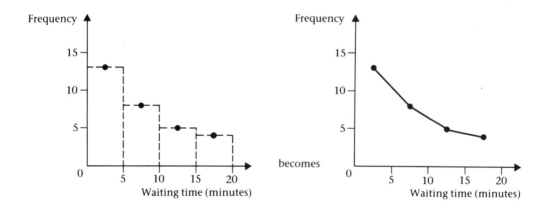

Draw the frequency polygon for Saturday.

Two frequency polygons can be shown on the same axes. A graph showing the frequency of values for data is also called the **distribution**.

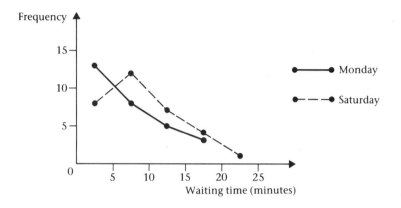

(a) Describe the main difference between the two distributions.

(b) Why might you have expected such a difference?

(c) What recommendation would you make to the manager of McTavish's on the basis of this evidence?

Frequency polygons are formed by plotting the mid-point of each group interval against its frequency and then joining the points with straight lines.

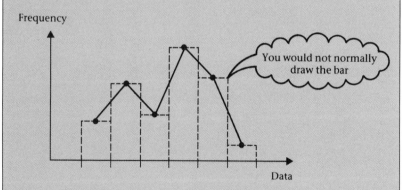

The advantage of the frequency polygon is that two (or more) data sets can be plotted on the same axes. This makes it easier to compare distributions.

EXERCISE 4

1   A college student carried out a survey to see if the television-watching habits for 17-year-old students were significantly different from those of 18-year-old students. He carried out a survey during the third week of May and asked fifty students in each group to record how much TV they watched during the week. The frequencies were:

Time watching TV (hours)	0–	5–	10–	15–	20–	25–	30–	35–40
17-year-olds	1	5	13	17	8	2	0	4
18-year-olds	6	20	14	9	0	1	0	0

(a) Show the data as two frequency polygons on a single set of axes.

(b) Compare the two distributions and explain why you might have expected the TV viewing habits to be different.

After working through this chapter you should:

1   know how to draw a frequency graph for:

   • qualitative data;

   • discrete data;

   • continuous data;

2   know when to use split bars (side-by-side or end-to-end);

3   know how to group discrete and continuous data in a sensible way without losing too much information;

4   know how to draw frequency polygons to compare distributions.

Grouped data

The following charts all show the same information: the amounts spent by 30 customers in McTavish's.

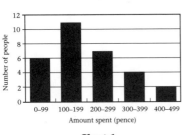

Chart 1

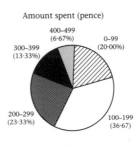

Chart 2

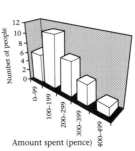

Chart 3

1 (a) Each of the charts shows the information in a different way. Use whichever is easiest to answer the following questions.

    (i) How many people spent £2 or more?

    (ii) What proportion spent less than £1?

    (iii) Which interval contains most people?

    (iv) Describe, in a few words, the way in which the amounts are distributed.

  (b) Which chart did you use to answer each question?

  (c) Which chart shows the information most clearly?

  (d) Comment on the strengths and weaknesses of each chart.

2 As well as showing the same information in different ways, different charts may also show different amounts of the original information. Draw up a table to show which information is available from each chart.

Information	Chart 1	Chart 2	Chart 3
Most anyone spent	Can be put between 400–499p		
Average amount spent			
Number spending at least £4			
Proportion spending less than £1			

See if you can now answer question 1(d) more fully.

3 Correlation

3.1 Two-way tables

A school has 120 sixth-form students. In the sixth form, games are optional and students can opt for other activities. A survey of the 120 students showed that 10 out of 50 boys had opted for other activities and that 49 girls had opted for games.

A student decides to show this information in a **two-way table**.

	Games	Other activities	Total
Boys		10	50
Girls	49		
Total			120

(a) How many boys opted for games?

(b) How many students altogether did **not** opt for games?

(c) 'More girls than boys opt for games so a girl is more likely to do games than a boy.' Do you agree with this conclusion?

(d) What conclusions (if any) can you draw?

Information gathered from a survey is often best illustrated by a two-way table if you wish to compare the responses to two questions.

A student investigating the different attitudes of boys and girls designed a questionnaire, from which the following is an extract.

> Boy   Girl
> • Are you a ☐   ☐   ? *Please tick the appropriate box*
>
> • How do you feel about maths?
>
>   (a) Like   ☐   *Tick the box*
>   (b) Dislike   ☐   *which describes*
>   (c) Neither like nor dislike   ☐   *how you feel*

In response to the two questions shown above, a student found that out of 254 pupils in year 10, 123 said they liked maths and 77 disliked it. There were 100 boys and of these 42 said they liked maths while only 38 said they disliked the subject.

(a) Show this information on a copy of the two-way table.

	Boy	Girl	Total
Like			
Dislike			
Neither			
Total			

(b) What percentage of boys dislike maths?

(c) What percentage of girls dislike maths?

(d) What conclusions can you draw?

(e) Give a reason why the two-way table is a good way of presenting the data.

(f) Comment on the design of the questionnaire.

EXERCISE 1

1 Henrik was on the catering committee of his college. He gave a questionnaire to 200 students from the college and obtained the following table on students' attitudes to college meals.

	Male	Female	Total
Like	?	?	?
Dislike	?	20	30
No opinion	40	30	?
Total	?	60	200

Copy and complete the table.

2 Students on a vocational course can opt for various different modules. They **must**, however, study either word processing (WP) or databases (DB) or both. A survey shows that of the 159 students on the course, 103 opted for word processing on its own while 47 opted for both subjects.

	WP	Not WP	Total
DB	47	a	
Not DB	b	c	
Total			159

(a) Explain why in the table $b = 103$ and $c = 0$.

(b) Copy and complete the table.

(c) How many students studied databases?

3 The results of an opinion poll of voters' intentions are shown in the table.

	Conservative	Labour	Liberal Democrat	Total
Male	232	179	83	
Female	217		141	
Total				1000

(a) Copy and complete the table.

(b) What percentage of Liberal Democrat voters are male?

(c) What percentage of males intend to vote Liberal Democrat?

4 In an experiment to compare two different ways of growing beans, a scientist recorded how many seeds germinated. She was called away before she could finish recording her results, but her assistant could see that there was enough information for him to complete the table for her.

	Method X	Method Y	Total
Germinated	12	13	25
Failed to germinate	13		
Total			55

(a) Copy and complete the table.

(b) What could you conclude from the evidence of this experiment?

5 In 1985–6 a survey revealed that the average person travelled approximately 100 miles per week. An investigation resulted in the following table of miles travelled:

	To and from work	Other reasons for travel	Total
Car	14	58	
Train	3	4	
Bus	2	4	
Other	7	8	
Total			100

(a) Copy the table and fill in the totals.

(b) What percentage of the distance travelled by train was for the purpose of going to and from work?

(c) What percentage of the distance travelled going to and from work was travelled by train?

6 20% of the workers employed by a local factory are men aged 30 or over and 35% are women aged under 30. Altogether, 55% of the workers are under 30. What percentage are women?

3.2 Scatter graphs

A student investigating circles measured the diameter and
circumference of various circular objects.

	Diameter x (cm)	Circumference y (cm)
Waste-paper basket	23·3	72·2
Plate	25·9	82·9
Jam jar	6·0	18·5
Cotton reel	2·4	8·2
Cereal bowl	13·4	42·8
Compact disc	12·0	38·2
Pencil	0·8	2·5

She decided to extend her investigation by taking these
measurements for the human head. She measured the
circumference just above the ears and took the diameter to be the
width of the head, again measured just above the ears.

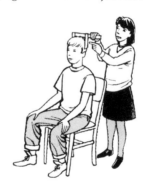

	Diameter x (cm)	Circumference y (cm)
Ann	14·8	56·3
Paul	16·0	55·8
Lisbeth	14·4	52·5
David	14·4	54·0
Rajesh	16·2	59·7
Sadia	15·1	55·1
Farah	15·3	57·0
Teresa	15·3	56·0

A **scatter graph** is a useful way of showing how two measurements might depend on each other. (Each pair of measurements is plotted as a single point.) The scatter graphs for the circle measurements and for the head measurements are as shown.

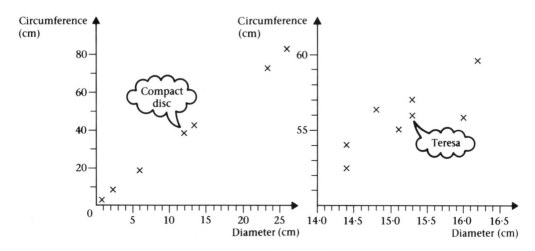

What similarities and what differences between the two situations are illustrated by the graphs? Give possible reasons for these similarities and differences.

Two related sets of measurements are said to be **correlated**. Sometimes the correlation is high. You would, for instance, expect a high correlation between inside leg measurement and height. A tall person is likely to have long legs and a short person is likely to have short legs. Although you might expect a similar relationship between inside leg measurement and weight, you would not expect it to be quite as strong. It would not be very unusual to find a few heavy people with short legs or a few light people with long legs. You can imagine the scatter graphs as looking something like this:

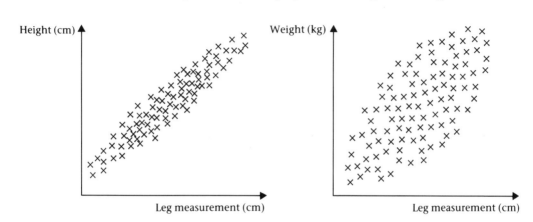

27

Qualities such as height, weight and leg measurement vary from person to person, so they are called **variables**.

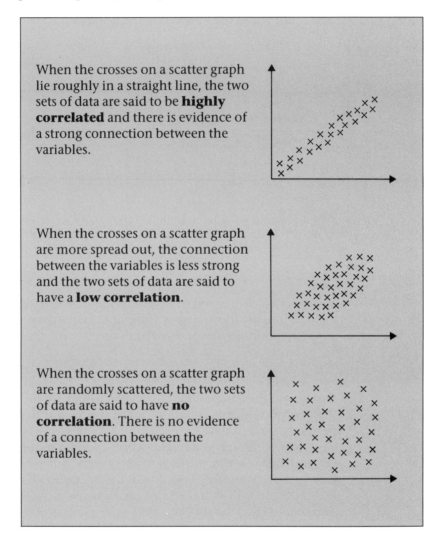

When the crosses on a scatter graph lie roughly in a straight line, the two sets of data are said to be **highly correlated** and there is evidence of a strong connection between the variables.

When the crosses on a scatter graph are more spread out, the connection between the variables is less strong and the two sets of data are said to have a **low correlation**.

When the crosses on a scatter graph are randomly scattered, the two sets of data are said to have **no correlation**. There is no evidence of a connection between the variables.

Draw a sketch of a scatter graph which shows the type of graph you would expect if you plotted:

(a) height against weight;

(b) arm length against leg length;

(c) head diameter against age for adults.

An apparent correlation does not **prove** that there is a connection between two variables. For example, storks migrate to Sweden from Africa each summer to breed. Research showed that the number of storks visiting Sweden was declining. Research also showed that over the same time period the birth rate in Sweden declined. In fact, when the data were plotted on a scatter graph, there was a very high correlation between the two data sets.

> Does this prove that storks bring babies?

A scatter graph may show a correlation. However, the graph does not prove anything if you cannot give a sensible reason **why** you should have expected a connection between the data sets.

Such a correlation is called a **spurious** correlation.

Sales of whisky (litres)

Teachers' salaries (£)

TASKSHEET 1 – *Looking for correlation (page 33)*

3.3 **Making predictions**

A local firm decides to manufacture cycle helmets. They decide to
market them in three sizes (small, medium and large). The question
is, how big should a 'medium' size be? The production manager
decides to do some research, collects data and draws a scatter graph.

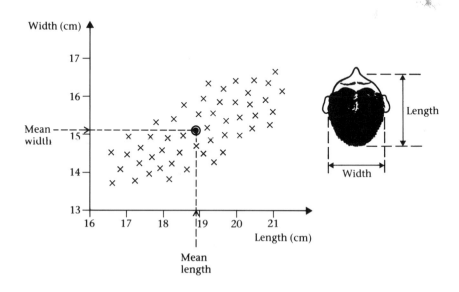

He calculates that the mean length is 18·8 cm and that the mean
width is 15·1 cm. He decides that this will be his recommended size
for the medium-sized helmet. He then decides that the small size
will have a length of 17·3 cm and that the large size will have a
length of 20·3 cm. (Adhesive pads can be used to ensure a snug fit for
other sizes.)

> (a) What widths would you recommend for small and large
>   helmets?
>
> (b) Describe the method you used to find these widths.

TASKSHEET 2 — Lines of best fit (page 35)

A **line of best fit** is a line which passes through the **mean point** of the scatter graph and follows the pattern of the points as closely as possible.

When there is a correlation between two data sets, x and y, you can use the line of best fit to predict an 'expected' value of y given an x-value.

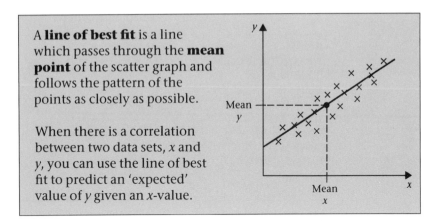

EXERCISE 2

1   A student decided to investigate whether there was a correlation between length of middle finger and length of arm. He measured seven friends and collected the following data.

| Finger length (cm) | 6·1 | 6·8 | 6·6 | 5·9 | 7·1 | 7·4 | 6·9 |
| Arm length (cm) | 51·5 | 70·5 | 63·0 | 53·0 | 69·5 | 76·0 | 58·0 |

(a) Why might the student have expected to find a correlation?

(b) Calculate the mean finger length and arm length.

(c) Plot the points on a scatter graph and draw the line of best fit.

(d) Describe the correlation.

(e) Use your line of best fit to estimate the arm length of a person whose finger length is known to be 7·9 cm.

2   A county under-16 girls' tennis squad attended an intensive training week. The coach timed each member for a 1000 m run at the start and end of the week to see how much (if any) improvement in general fitness had taken place.

| Time at start (s) | 365 | 342 | 408 | 391 | 301 | 285 | 286 | 331 |
| Time at end (s) | 342 | 346 | 372 | 373 | 289 | 287 | 281 | 315 |

One of the girls had to leave a day early. Her time at the start of the week was 328 seconds. Draw a scatter graph and use it to estimate what her time would have been if she had stayed to the end.

3 A police cadet is doing some research into the link between crime and unemployment and compiles the following table.

	Unemployment (%)*	Crime rate#
North	9·6	10·3
Yorks & Humberside	8·0	8·4
E. Midlands	6·1	7·1
E. Anglia	5·1	5·6
South East	5·2	7·7
South West	6·1	6·0
W. Midlands	6·9	7·0
North West	8·4	8·9
Wales	7·8	6·9
Scotland	8·5	9·7

*Figures for Jan 1991. *Regional Trends 26* (1991), table 2.5
#Total notifiable offences recorded by police in 1989. Rates per 100 population.
Regional Trends 26 (1991), table 8.1

(a) Display the information on a scatter graph and draw the line of best fit.

(b) Use your line of best fit to estimate the likely crime rate in a region where unemployment is 14%.

(c) Northern Ireland has 14·1% unemployment and a crime rate of 3·5%. Comment on this in relation to the information given in the table.

After working through this chapter you should:

1 know how to display data in a two-way table;

2 know how to draw conclusions from data displayed in a two-way table;

3 know what a scatter graph is and how to describe the correlation between two variables given a scatter graph;

4 know how to construct a line of best fit on a scatter graph.

Looking for correlation

The following data were collected for 20 students in a maths class.

Name	Score in maths (%)	Leg length (cm)	Time for 100 m (s)	Long jump (m)
Alan	97	73	14·5	3·27
Sandra	72	78	13·4	4·00
Barry	68	77	14·1	3·95
Ann	97	69	14·0	3·72
Karen	84	70	14·7	3·57
John	62	75	14·4	3·43
Fatima	72	78	13·9	4·25
John	69	78	14·8	4·11
Peter	63	74	15·9	3·05
Latif	100	72	16·1	3·23
Malik	40	79	13·3	4·25
Lyn	82	81	15·2	4·07
Rosi	59	78	13·6	4·05
Jane	45	82	13·7	3·92
Rabia	54	74	13·7	3·41
David	95	76	14·2	3·80
Winston	93	77	13·0	3·80
Sabera	61	76	15·2	4·13
Bjorn	70	81	13·3	4·71
Gareth	70	79	15·5	4·23
Mean	72·65	76·35	14·325	3·8475

1   What type of correlation would you expect to find between the measurements for leg length and for the long jump? Explain why. Draw a scatter graph and comment on what you find.

2   Draw a scatter graph to show the correlation between the measurements for the 100 m sprint and the long jump. In what way does this graph differ from that of question 1? Explain why you would expect this type of relationship.

3   Draw and comment on the scatter graph for maths scores and leg lengths.

4   The table shows the life expectancy of people in a variety of countries, and each country's gross domestic product (GDP), which is a measure of its wealth.

	Life expectancy	Per capita GDP ($000s)
Afghanistan	42	0·1
Bangladesh	51	0·2
Czechoslovakia	72	2·7
France	76	17·0
Greece	76	5·2
India	58	0·3
Indonesia	56	0·5
Italy	76	14·4
Japan	78	23·3
Kenya	59	0·3
Nigeria	51	0·3
Pakistan	57	0·4
Philippines	64	0·7
Poland	72	1·7
Sierra Leone	41	0·2
Sweden	77	21·1
Turkey	65	1·4
UK	75	14·5
USA	76	19·8
Vietnam	63	0·2
W. Germany	75	19·7

The Economist Book of Vital World Statistics, 1990

Draw a scatter graph for this information. Is there a correlation between life expectancy in a country and its per capita GDP?

Lines of best fit

Consider again the data collected by the student featured at the start of section 3.2. You may recall that she was investigating the relationship between circumference and diameter and collected the following data.

Data set I		Data set II	
Diameter x (cm)	Circumference y (cm)	Diameter x (cm)	Circumference y (cm)
23·3	72·2	14·8	56·3
25·9	82·9	16·0	55·8
6·0	18·5	14·4	52·5
2·4	8·2	14·4	54·0
13·4	42·8	16·2	59·7
12·0	38·2	15·1	55·1
0·8	2·5	15·3	57·0
		15·3	56·0

1 Plot the scatter graph for each of the data sets.

2 For each scatter graph draw a straight line which you think 'looks' best (i.e. follows the pattern of the points as closely as possible). This line is called the line of best fit.

3 For the first data set, use the line of best fit to estimate:

(a) y when $x = 9$ cm; (b) x when $y = 60$ cm.

4 For the second data set, use the line of best fit to estimate:

(a) y when $x = 14·7$ cm; (b) x when $y = 58$ cm.

5 For the first data set calculate the mean (average) value of x and of y. These two values can be plotted as a single point on the scatter graph. Plot the mean point on the scatter graph.

6 Calculate the mean point of the second data set and plot it on the scatter graph.

4 An average value

4.1 What is average?

It is terrible! 25% of children are below average! We must improve standards. The government's aim is for **all** children to be above average!

There are lies, damned lies and statistics (Benjamin Disraeli).

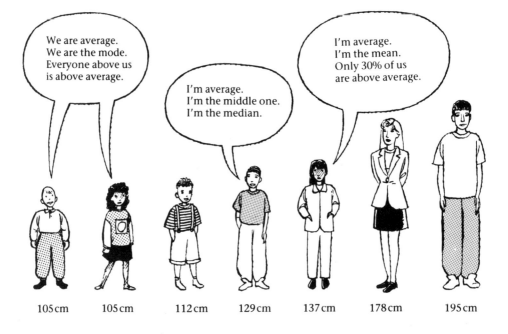

We are average.
We are the mode.
Everyone above us
is above average.

I'm average.
I'm the middle one.
I'm the median.

I'm average.
I'm the mean.
Only 30% of us
are above average.

105 cm   105 cm   112 cm   129 cm   137 cm   178 cm   195 cm

(a) What do you think politicians mean by the word 'average'?

(b) What do you think Disraeli meant by the word 'statistic'?

(c) The **mean, median** and **mode** are all averages. They all have different values for the children shown in the cartoon. Discuss how you think these averages are defined.

(d) Disraeli referred to lies. A boy claims to have evidence which shows that boys are, on average, better at learning facts than girls. What questions would you ask before you were prepared to accept his claim as being true?

If something is said to be average, it is important to know which average is being referred to.

> The term 'average' can refer to one of three different statistics:
>
> • **The mean**: found by adding up all the data items and dividing by the number of items in the data set;
>
> • **The median**: the middle data item when the data set is put in rank order. (If the middle falls between two data items, then the median is taken to be half-way between them.)
>
> • **The mode**: the data item that occurs most often in a data set.

TASKSHEET 1 — Mean, median and mode (page 45)

EXAMPLE 1

A supermarket manager was considering whether the car-park at the back of the store needed to be larger. He asked one of his Saturday assistants to record the number of cars entering the car-park during each of the 12 successive five-minute periods from 10 a.m. to 11 a.m. The numbers of cars were:

3 0 2 5 2 5 2 1 6 7 0 4

Find the mean, median and mode.

SOLUTION

Mean: $\dfrac{3 + 0 + 2 + 5 + 2 + 5 + 2 + 1 + 6 + 7 + 0 + 4}{12} = \dfrac{37}{12} = 3{\cdot}08$ cars

Median: The data set arranged in order becomes:

0 0 1 2 2 ② ③ 4 5 5 6 7

There are two middle values (shown circled). The median is taken to be mid-way between these, so the median is 2·5 cars.

Mode: The most frequently occurring data item is 2 cars.

TASKSHEET   2E   –   Pooling data (page 47)

EXERCISE   1

1 The sums of money spent by nine 17-year-olds on a Saturday night out were as follows:

£5   £5   £10   £25   £5   £8   £7   £10   £15

Find the mean, median and mode.

2 One afternoon the children's department of a sports shop sold ten of a certain style of T-shirt. The sizes (in inches) of the shirts sold were:

28   30   30   32   34   36   38   38   38   40

(a) Find the mean, median and mode.

(b) Why might the shopkeeper consider the mode to be the most useful measure of average?

3 A shoe shop sells an average 230 pairs of shoes per week at an average profit of £4·50 per pair. So the total profit per week is:

£4·50 × 230 = £1035

Which measure of average is the shopkeeper using in this calculation? Explain your answer.

4 Datasheet 1 shows an end-of-season league table.

(a) Calculate the mean number of 'goals for'.

(b) Calculate the mean number of 'goals against'.

(c) Explain why your answers to (a) and (b) should be the same.

5E As part of its staff training programme, a company employs a consultant to run courses in time management. During a course, each member of the group is asked to estimate one minute. There are six groups. The table shows the size of each group and the mean estimate for each group.

Group name	A	B	C	D	E	F
Number of trainees	17	21	18	22	19	23
Mean estimate (seconds)	53	62	58	52	61	55

Pool the results and calculate the mean value for **all** the trainees.

4.2 Dealing with repetition

The table shows the results of the third round of the FA Cup played in January 1992.

FA CUP – Third Round
Results Service
Matches played January 1992

Home Team		Away Team	
Aston Villa	0	Tottenham Hotspur	0
Blackburn Rovers	4	Kettering Town	1
Bristol Rovers	5	Plymouth Argyle	0
Bolton Wanderers	2	Reading	0
Bournemouth	0	Newcastle United	0
Brighton & Hove Albion	5	Crawley Town	0
Bristol City	1	Wimbledon	1
Burnley	2	Derby County	2
Charlton Athletic	3	Barnet	1
Coventry City	1	Cambridge United	1
Crewe Alexander	0	Liverpool	4
Everton	1	Southend United	0
Exeter City	1	Portsmouth	2
Farnborough Town	1	West Ham United	1
Huddersfield Town	0	Millwall	4
Hull City	0	Chelsea	2
Ipswich Town	1	Hartlepool United	1
Leeds United	0	Manchester United	1
Leicester City	1	Crystal Palace	0
Middlesbrough	2	Manchester City	1
Norwich City	1	Barnsley	0
Nottingham Forest	1	Wolverhampton Wanderers	0
Notts County	2	Wigan Athletic	0
Oldham Athletic	1	Leyton Orient	1
Oxford United	3	Tranmere Rovers	1
Preston North End	0	Sheffield Wednesday	2
Sheffield United	4	Luton Town	0
Southampton	2	Queens Park Rangers	0
Sunderland	3	Port Vale	0
Swindon Town	3	Watford	2
Woking	0	Hereford United	0
Wrexham	2	Arsenal	1

64 football teams took part, so to calculate the mean number of goals scored per team, you can add up all the goals and divide by 64.

$$\frac{0 + 4 + 5 + 2 + 0 + 5 + 1 + 2 \ldots}{64}$$

Use this method to calculate the mean.

The mean can be calculated very quickly if you have a frequency table.

Goals x	Frequency f
0	22
1	21
2	11
3	4
4	4
5	2

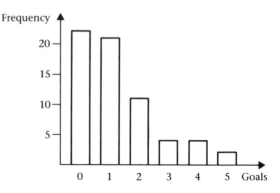

The table shows that the data item 2 occurred with a frequency of 11. This means that 11 teams scored two goals and so their contribution to the total number of goals scored is $2 \times 11 = 22$ goals. This is quicker than, but just the same as, adding 2 to itself 11 times.

(a) Use the frequency table to explain why the total number of goals is:

$(0 \times 22) + (1 \times 21) + (2 \times 11) + (3 \times 4) + (4 \times 4) + (5 \times 2)$

(b) Explain how you can use the frequency table to calculate the total number of teams taking part.

(c) Calculate the mean number of goals per team.

(d) Explain how you can use the frequency table to calculate the median number of goals scored.

To calculate the mean from a frequency table, you:

- calculate the number of data items by adding together all the frequencies;

- calculate the total of all the data items by multiplying each number by its frequency and then adding these results together;

- calculate the mean by dividing the total of all the data items by the number of data items.

EXAMPLE 2

A group of parents claimed that the road their children had to cross to get to school was dangerous. The local authority did a traffic survey and compiled a frequency table on the number of cars passing a certain point each minute.

Number of cars	2	3	4	5	6	7
Frequency	3	7	15	10	3	2

(a) For how many one-minute intervals were data recorded?

(b) How many cars passed altogether?

(c) Calculate the mean number of cars passing per minute.

SOLUTION

Number of cars x	Frequency f	$x \times f$
2	3	6
3	7	21
4	15	60
5	10	50
6	3	18
7	2	14
Total	40	169

(a) Data were collected for 40 one-minute intervals.

(b) 169 cars passed the point during this time.

(c) The mean was $169 \div 40 = 4 \cdot 225$ cars per minute.

EXERCISE 2

1 In a survey into the diet of young people, students from a college were asked how many times in the last week they had eaten chips with their main meals. The results were:

Number of meals with chips	0	1	2	3	4	5	6	7
Frequency	5	8	25	49	51	37	17	8

(a) How many students took part in the survey?

(b) Calculate the mean number of times per week that a student from the college had chips.

4.3 Grouped data

You may recall from chapter 2 that the researcher at McTavish's restaurant collected data on how long customers had to wait before being served. The frequency table and graph for Monday are as shown.

Waiting time t (minutes)	0–	5–	10–	15–20
Frequency f	13	8	5	4

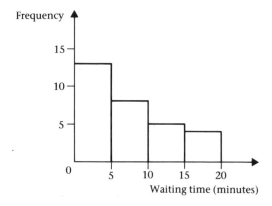

You can see from the table that four customers had to wait between 15 and 20 minutes. When data are grouped like this, information is 'lost' and you cannot put a precise figure on how long each customer had to wait. You can, however, say that the four customers each had to wait **about** 17·5 minutes, which gives a total of $4 \times 17·5 = 70$ minutes spent waiting.

(a) Why is this a reasonable estimate?

(b) About how long did the eight customers who each waited between 5 and 10 minutes spend waiting in total?

(c) Use this method to calculate a reasonable estimate of the total time spent waiting by all the customers in the survey.

(d) How many customers were involved in the survey?

(e) Use your answers to (c) and (d) to calculate an estimate of the mean time customers spent waiting to be served.

> When calculating the mean from a frequency table of grouped data, take the mid-point of each interval to represent the interval and multiply it by the interval frequency.

EXAMPLE 3

The table shows the weight distribution of a hundred 17-year-old boys, selected at random.

Weight w (kg)	50–	60–	70–	80–90
Frequency f	9	59	25	7

Calculate the mean weight.

SOLUTION

Take the mid-point of each group interval as representative of the group.

Mid-point w	Frequency f	$w \times f$
55	9	495
65	59	3835
75	25	1875
85	7	595
Total	100	6800

Mean weight $= \frac{6800}{100} = 68 \, \text{kg}$

> A student tried to answer the question above by saying that as there are four data items (55, 65, 75 and 85) the mean should be $6800 \div 4 = 1700 \, \text{kg}$.
>
> Why is this obviously wrong?

TASKSHEET 3 – *Changing intervals (page 48)*

EXERCISE 3

1 Students took part in an obstacle race as part of a fund-raising day. The times taken to complete the race are given in the frequency table.

Time (s)	40–	50–	60–	70–	80–	90–100
Frequency	1	5	23	47	13	1

(a) How many students took part in the race?

(b) Calculate the mean time for completing the course.

2 Kim goes to work by bus at the same time each day. The journey should take 23 minutes according to the timetable. It seems as though it always takes longer, so she starts to keep a careful record of how long the journey actually takes. Her results are:

Time (minutes)	20–	25–	30–	35–	40–45
Frequency	2	6	18	4	0

(a) For how many days did she keep a record?

(b) Calculate the mean time for the journey.

3 Mukul kept a record of daily rainfall for a number of days.

Rainfall (mm)	0–	4–	8–	12–	16–	20–	24–	28–32
Frequency (days)	25	12	7	15	2	0	5	1

(a) Calculate the mean rainfall per day.

(b) Use your answer to (a) to estimate the annual rainfall.

(c) Comment on whether this is likely to be a good estimate.

After working through this chapter, you should:

1 know that there are three types of average commonly used:

- the mean,
- the median,
- the mode;

2 know how to calculate the mean, median and mode for a data set which has not been grouped;

3 know how to calculate the mean when the data set is given in a frequency table.

Mean, median and mode

1

Mode   Median   Mean

Mean   = 137·3 cm
Median = 129 cm
Mode   = 105 cm

105 cm   105 cm   112 cm   129 cm   137 cm   178 cm   195 cm

An eighth child joins this line. His height is 150 cm. What difference does he make to:

(a) the mean;   (b) the median;   (c) the mode?

2 Cricket scores from the last nine innings of a batsman are:

14   22   3   48   71   27   1   102   11

(a) What is his total score for all nine innings?

(b) Calculate the mean score per innings.

(c) These data have no mode. Explain why this is the case.

(d) The median might mistakenly be taken to be 71. Why?

(e) What is the median score?

In his next innings the batsman scores a 'duck', meaning he does not score any runs.

(f) Calculate the new value of the mean.

(g) There is now no middle item of data, but the median is taken to be 18. Explain why.

The batsman has no better luck in his next innings and scores another duck, so his mode is now 0.

(h) Explain why the mode is not the most appropriate statistic to use as an average in this case.

(i) Would you select the mean or the median as the most appropriate statistic to represent the batsman's performance? Explain your answer.

3 In a small business, the managing director has a salary of £35 000 and the production manager has a salary of £25 000. The salaries of five members of staff are £12 000, £14 500, £15 500, £17 000 and £19 000 while a further four members of staff each receive £13 500.

(a) Find the mean, the median and the mode of the salaries.

All staff negotiate for a pay rise with the board of directors.

(b) Explain why, if the average salary is to be used as a basis for negotiation, it is in the board's interest to use the mean, whereas it is in the staff's interest to use the mode.

(c) Which average do you think should be used? (Give a reason.)

4 The gross domestic product of each of ten African countries for the year 1988 was as shown.

South Africa	87·55	Kenya	7·39	Morocco	18·52	Zaire	6·47
Zimbabwe	4·60	Tunisia	10·05	Nigeria	30·10	Chad	0·86
Mozambique	1·17	Botswana	1·80				

The Economist Book of Vital World Statistics
(All figures are in billions of US dollars;
the figure for the UK is 826·32.)

(a) Find the mean and median gross domestic product.

The gross domestic products for the three countries of North America were:

USA   4881·00   Canada   488·75   Mexico   173·93

(b) Find the mean and median gross domestic product.

An Oxfam campaigner wants to use average gross domestic product in a comparison of Africa and North America.

(c) Which statistic would you advise the campaigner to use? Explain your choice.

Pooling data

In statistics, a larger sample can often be obtained by pooling the data from two or more smaller data sets. If the mean of each data set is known then the mean of the pooled set can be calculated from them.

1 A class of 12 girls and 6 boys take a test. In discussing the test, the teacher tells the class that the mean mark was 38·4 for the girls but only 34·6 for the boys. (The mean is rounded to one decimal place.) The teacher challenges the class to find the mean for the whole class from this information.

Dave (incorrectly!) suggests the mean for the whole class should be 36·5 as this is the mean of 38·4 and 34·6.

Sue works out that the total mark for all the girls must be 461.

(a) What calculation has she done?

(b) What is the total mark for all the boys?

(c) What is the total mark for the whole class?

(d) What is the mean for the whole class?

2 A minibus company needs to 'average' 12 passengers per run between the station and the shopping centre at peak times in order to be profitable. The bus does ten runs during the peak period and the driver notes how many passengers are carried on each journey. Before starting on her final run, the bus driver notes that the number of passengers carried so far is:

    9   10   13   14   15   15   11   11   9

(a) What is the mean number of passengers per run for these first nine runs?

(b) How many passengers are needed on the tenth run to give a mean average of 12 passengers per run?

(c) If instead of the mean, 'average' is taken to refer to the median, how many passengers are needed on the tenth run to give an average of 12 passengers per run?

(d) Do you think the minibus company is referring to a mean or to a median when it talks of the 'average' number of passengers?

Changing intervals

Three different students working together on a statistics project selected 100 girls at random and recorded their weights.

The students devised different questionnaires. Mary recorded the actual weight in kilograms of each girl. Her results were:

62·7	67·6	65·2	64·5	57·0	62·7	66·0	65·3	59·2	69·4
62·8	59·5	63·9	58·0	72·6	60·0	61·5	75·0	66·5	59·9
60·7	63·5	65·6	67·1	66·1	62·6	64·2	65·2	60·7	57·6
73·0	65·3	62·3	63·5	67·0	62·6	44·7	57·6	61·8	44·7
47·8	61·0	66·4	61·4	47·8	55·6	61·0	64·8	63·1	64·7
50·9	63·4	64·0	58·9	65·0	61·3	58·6	59·4	66·9	61·8
60·6	75·0	59·7	64·5	60·8	63·1	59·3	63·9	47·8	61·3
68·9	59·9	61·9	66·7	44·7	62·1	63·2	66·6	60·4	68·1
51·9	63·3	62·9	61·6	59·3	67·4	76·3	67·3	64·6	63·5
60·0	58·0	76·3	62·3	49·6	64·4	67·3	62·5	60·8	59·7

1   Calculate the mean weight.

Joan and Maggie recorded the results on tally charts which grouped the weights in different ways. Their results are summarised in the following tables.

Weight w (kg)	Frequency f
$40 \leqslant w < 45$	3
$45 \leqslant w < 50$	4
$50 \leqslant w < 55$	2
$55 \leqslant w < 60$	17
$60 \leqslant w < 65$	46
$65 \leqslant w < 70$	22
$70 \leqslant w < 75$	2
$75 \leqslant w < 80$	4

Weight w (kg)	Frequency f
$40 \leqslant w < 50$	7
$50 \leqslant w < 60$	19
$60 \leqslant w < 70$	68
$70 \leqslant w < 80$	6

2   (a)   Use the first table to calculate the mean weight.

   (b)   Use the second table to calculate the mean weight.

   (c)   Comment on any discrepancy between your answers to questions 1, 2(a) and 2(b).

5 Measures of spread

5.1 Cumulative frequency

357 athletes competed in a fell race run over a distance of 8 miles. The finishing times of the athletes, in minutes, are shown in the frequency table.

Time (minutes)	60–	70–	80–	90–	100–	110–	120–	130–140
Number of athletes	2	14	31	59	108	84	42	17

(a) How many runners completed the course in under $1\frac{1}{2}$ hours?

(b) Estimate the time taken by the median runner (the runner who finished 179th).

These data can be presented both in a **cumulative frequency table** and as a **cumulative frequency graph**.

Time (minutes) less than	70	80	90	100	110	120	130	140
Number of athletes		2	16	47	106	214	298	340	357

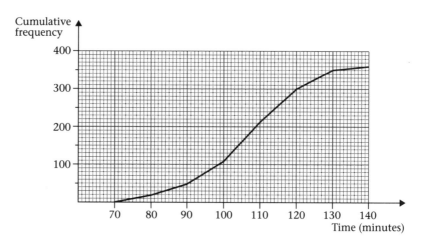

- A frequency is the number of items of data in a particular group interval.

- A cumulative frequency is the total number of items of data up to a particular value.

(a) Explain how the cumulative frequency table has been obtained from the frequency table.

(b) The cumulative frequency table shows that 100 minutes has a cumulative frequency of 106. Explain what this means.

(c) Explain how the cumulative frequency graph has been obtained from the cumulative frequency table.

(d) Discuss how you can use the cumulative frequency graph to estimate the median.

(e) Discuss how you can use the graph to estimate how many runners took between 85 and 105 minutes to complete the race.

TASKSHEET 1 — Cumulative frequency (page 58)

EXAMPLE 1

188 students from year 11 in a school sat a geography exam. The distribution of their marks is shown in the frequency table.

Mark	20–	30–	40–	50–	60–	70–	80–	90–100
Frequency	3	7	14	26	62	37	26	13

(a) Draw a cumulative frequency graph for the data.

(b) Use the graph to estimate the median mark.

SOLUTION

(a)

Upper limit	Cumulative frequency
30	3
40	10
50	24
60	50
70	112
80	149
90	175
100	188

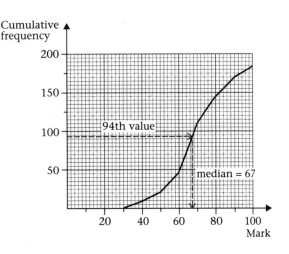

(b) $\frac{1}{2} \times 188 = 94$. You can see from the graph that the median mark is 67. (Strictly, the median is mid-way between the 94th and the 95th mark, so you should read off the mark which corresponds to a cumulative frequency of 94·5. However, this has no noticeable effect on the answer.)

(a) 25% of the students gained a grade A. What is the minimum mark needed for an A grade?

(b) 25% of students failed the exam. What was the pass mark?

5.2 Quartiles

You have seen how the median divides the sample into two halves. In a similar way, **quartiles** divide the data set into quarters.

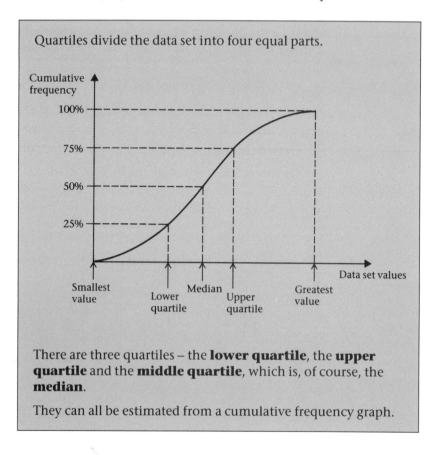

Quartiles divide the data set into four equal parts.

There are three quartiles – the **lower quartile**, the **upper quartile** and the **middle quartile**, which is, of course, the **median**.

They can all be estimated from a cumulative frequency graph.

For small samples, you calculate the quartiles in the same way as the median by first putting the data in rank order.

- To find the lower quartile, find the median of the data items **below** the median value.
- To find the upper quartile, find the median of the data items **above** the median value.

EXAMPLE 2

The following data set shows the widths (in centimetres) of the thumb nails of twelve people selected at random.

2·2   1·7   1·1   1·2   2·5   1·4   1·2   2·0
1·3   1·3   1·7   1·5

(a) Find the median.

(b) Find the upper and lower quartiles.

SOLUTION

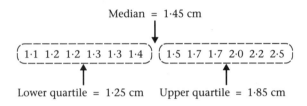

EXERCISE 1

1   Find the median and the upper and lower quartiles for this data set (the scores made by the eleven players in a recent cricket match).

31   32   11   9   4   56   52   18   13   21   1

2   For her project, Jafar was investigating family size. Ten of her friends gave her the following data for the numbers of children in their families.

3   2   4   2   1   3   2   2   5   3

Find the median and the upper and lower quartiles.

3   The frequency table shows the annual income, in £000s, for 200 people selected at random for an economics survey.

Income (£000s)	0–	4–	8–	12–	16–	20–	24–	28–32
Frequency	5	24	45	56	37	19	11	3

(a) Construct the cumulative frequency table and draw the graph for these data.

(b) Use the graph to estimate the median, the upper and the lower quartiles.

5.3 Spread

The three data sets on datasheet 2 are the weights, in kilograms, of:

- A – 30 babies born at the maternity unit last month;
- B – 30 fish caught in a local angling competition;
- C – the prize-winning marrow at 30 local vegetable shows.

For each of the data sets A, B and C:

(a) calculate the mean;   (b) find the median.

What do you notice about these statistics?

The frequency polygons show the frequency distributions for the three data sets on datasheet 2.

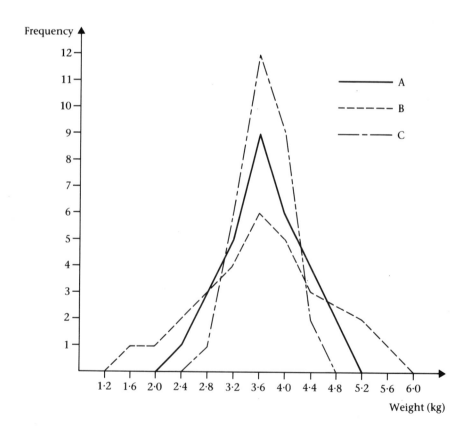

(a) Use the frequency polygons to describe how the spreads of the three data sets differ.

(b) Suggest a statistic to measure the spread of data sets such as those shown.

Consider again the data for the 357 athletes who competed in the eight-mile fell race.

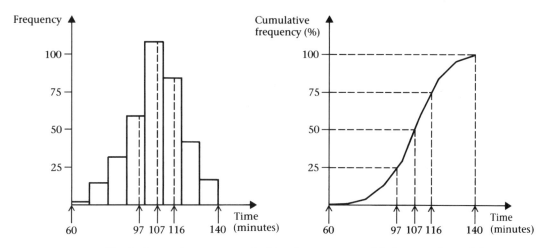

Only five values are needed to give a reasonable impression of the **spread** of the times taken to complete the race.

- The fastest time   60 minutes
- The lower quartile   97 minutes
- The median   107 minutes
- The upper quartile   116 minutes
- The slowest time   140 minutes

The spread of data can be described using either:

- the **range** – the difference between the smallest and the largest data item;

- the **interquartile range** – the difference between the lower quartile and the upper quartile.

Calculate estimates of the range and the interquartile range for the fell race data.

5.4 Box and whisker diagrams

Once you have calculated the quartiles of a data set it is easy to draw a **box and whisker diagram**. For example, the distribution of data for the fell race is represented as shown.

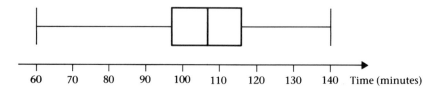

(a) Which parts of the data form the box?

(b) Which parts of the data form the whiskers?

(c) How is the range shown?

(d) How is the interquartile range shown?

Box and whisker diagrams are useful for comparing different data sets.

E X A M P L E 3

The box and whisker diagrams show the pulse rates for two groups of students.

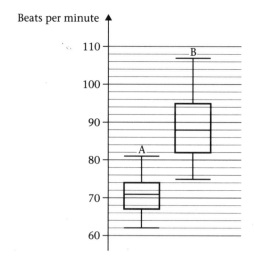

Compare the two groups and comment on the possible reasons for the differences in spread.

SOLUTION

	Smallest value	LQ	Median	UQ	Largest value	Range	IQR
Group A	62	67	71	74	81	19	7
Group B	75	82	88	95	107	32	13

(LQ = Lower quartile,   UQ = Upper quartile,   IQR = Interquartile range)

A pulse of 70 is typical for a relaxed healthy adult. It would be reasonable to assume this is a fair description of group A. The students in group B have a higher median pulse and the data are more spread out. There are many possible reasons for this. For example, it could be that students in this group have recently taken part in some form of physical activity.

> Draw box and whisker diagrams for the questions in exercise 1.

After working through this chapter you should:

1   know what cumulative frequency means;

2   know how to plot a cumulative frequency graph;

3   know how to obtain information from a cumulative frequency graph;

4   know what upper and lower quartiles are;

5   know what the terms range and interquartile range mean, and understand how these statistics are used to describe the spread of a data set;

6   know how to construct and interpret a box and whisker diagram.

Cumulative frequency

The frequency distribution for the weights of 100 17-year-old boys is:

Weight (kg)	55–	60–	65–	70–	75–	80–	85–90
Frequency	4	9	15	25	28	14	5

The table shows that 15 boys weigh between 65 and 70 kg. Although you do not know what the boys' individual weights are, you can conclude that they all weigh **less than** 70 kg.

1 How many boys altogether weigh:

(a) less than 70 kg;   (b) less than 60 kg?

2 Complete the cumulative frequency table:

Weight (kg)	60	65	70	75	80	85	90
Cumulative frequency	4	13	28				

3 (a) How many boys weigh less than 90 kg?

(b) Explain why your answer to (a) should agree with the total frequency.

4 If you were asked to calculate an estimate of the mean, you would use the mid-point values of each interval. Explain why you do not use the mid-point value to construct a cumulative frequency table.

5 Draw a cumulative frequency graph from your cumulative frequency table by plotting the points on a suitable set of axes and joining the points with straight lines.

6 Use the cumulative frequency graph to estimate:

(a) the median weight;

(b) how many boys weigh less than 72 kg;

(c) how many boys weigh between 62 and 82 kg.

6 Probability

6.1 Types of probability

In a cricket match it can be very important to win the toss and therefore be able to choose who should bat first.

A coin is tossed at the start of a cricket match because both sides agree that tossing a coin is fair; both sides have an equal chance of winning the toss.

(a) Explain why it is reasonable to assume that a coin will land heads or tails with equal probability.

(b) What is the probability that a coin lands heads?

(c) At the start of a tennis match, one of the players spins a racket to see who serves first. Is this a fair way of deciding? Explain your answer.

(d) An umpire of a cricket match forgets to bring a coin. He suggests that he spins a cricket bat and that one of the captains calls out 'front' or 'back'. Is this fair?

 TASKSHEET 1 – Investigating probability (page 68)

The probability of an event happening is based on one of two ideas:

- The mathematical idea of symmetry – the two faces of a coin are equally likely so the probability of its landing heads uppermost is 1 in 2 or $\frac{1}{2}$.

- 'Relative frequency' obtained from past experience – for example, an experiment may show you that a cricket bat lands front face up on 20 out of 30 occasions. The relative frequency is $\frac{20}{30}$ or $\frac{2}{3}$. This can be used as an estimate of probability.

When you predict the likelihood or chance of something happening, you make a statement about its **probability**. The probability of a coin landing heads can be expressed in a number of different ways:

     50–50   1 in 2   50% $\frac{1}{2}$ 0·5

In this chapter you will see that it is usually best to express probabilities as fractions or as decimals.

The chance of some event happening can be any value from zero probability (no chance) to a probability of one (certain to happen).

Probability line

Copy the probability line and mark on the probability of:

(a) getting a six when you throw a die;

(b) **not** getting a six when you throw a die;

(c) getting a spade when you pick a card from a well-shuffled pack;

(d) an American tennis player winning the women's championship at Wimbledon next year. Justify your answer.

6.2 Adding probabilities

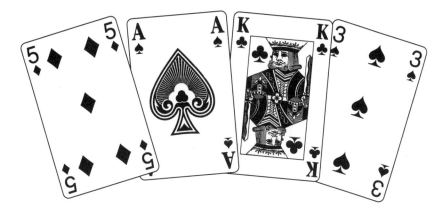

Some events are **mutually exclusive**. If two events are mutually exclusive then they cannot both occur at the same time.

For instance, when you pick a card at random from a standard pack of 52 playing cards several events are possible. The event 'the card is a club' and the event 'the card is a diamond' are mutually exclusive as no single card fits both descriptions. On the other hand, the event 'the card is a club' and the event 'the card is an ace' are not mutually exclusive as there is a card which fits both descriptions. The two events overlap.

> Which card fits both the event 'the card is a club' and the event 'the card is an ace'?

TASKSHEET 2 — Adding probabilities (page 70)

> If two events A and B are **mutually exclusive**, then:
>
> $$P(A \text{ or } B) = P(A) + P(B)$$
>
> where $P(A)$ is the probability of event A occurring and $P(A \text{ or } B)$ is the probability of **either A or B** occurring.

EXAMPLE 1

In a restaurant, customers order for their main course meat (event A), fish (event B) or a vegetarian meal (event C). The waiter estimates from experience that 50% of customers order meat and that 30% order fish. What is the probability that the next customer orders either meat or fish?

SOLUTION

$P(A) = 0·5$ and $P(B) = 0·3$

The two events are mutually exclusive so:

$$P(A \text{ or } B) = P(A) + P(B)$$
$$= 0·5 + 0·3$$
$$= 0·8$$

If two or more events cover all possible outcomes, then they are **exhaustive**. In the example, the mutually exclusive events A, B and C are exhaustive and so 20% of customers order a vegetarian meal.

> If the mutually exclusive events A, B, C . . . cover all possible outcomes, then:
>
> $$P(A) + P(B) + P(C) + \ldots = 1$$

A particularly important case is the probability of an event **not** occurring.

> $$P(\text{not } A) = 1 - P(A)$$

In example 1, find:

(a) P(not B);   (b) P(A or C);   (c) P(A or B or C);

(d) P(B or not B).

6.3 Multiplying probabilities

Some events are **independent**. If two events are independent then the fact that one has occurred does not change the probability that the other may occur.

For instance, it would be reasonable to assume that the two events 'Mary wins a prize in the raffle' and 'Mary is late for work' are independent. On the other hand, it would **not** be reasonable to assume that the two events 'Mary is late for work' and 'Mary's car breaks down' are independent.

> (a) Would it be reasonable to assume that the two events 'Mary wins a prize in the raffle' and 'Mary's car breaks down' are independent?
>
> (b) Are these events mutually exclusive?

TASKSHEET 3 — Multiplying probabilities (page 71)

> If two events A and B are **independent**, then:
>
> P(A and B) = P(A) × P(B)
>
> where P(A and B) is the probability that **both** events occur.

EXAMPLE 2

After a cycle safety check it was found that $\frac{3}{5}$ of bicycles had faulty brakes. It was also noted that $\frac{1}{4}$ of bicycles were blue.

What is the probability that a bicycle selected at random:

(a) has faulty brakes **and** is blue;

(b) does not have faulty brakes and is blue?

SOLUTION

If event A is 'faulty brakes', then $P(A) = \frac{3}{5}$ and $P(\text{not } A) = \frac{2}{5}$

If event B is 'coloured blue', then $P(B) = \frac{1}{4}$ and $P(\text{not } B) = \frac{3}{4}$

(a) $P(A \text{ and } B) = P(A) \times P(B) = \frac{3}{5} \times \frac{1}{4} = \frac{3}{20}$

(b) $P(\text{not } A \text{ and } B) = P(\text{not } A) \times P(B) = \frac{2}{5} \times \frac{1}{4} = \frac{2}{20} = \frac{1}{10}$

What assumption has been made in the solution above?

EXERCISE 1

1 A bag has 3 red and 5 black counters. A second bag has 5 red and 7 black counters. Two counters are taken at random, one from each bag. What is the probability that both counters are red?

2 The probability that someone is left-handed is $\frac{2}{9}$ and the probability that someone wears glasses is $\frac{3}{10}$. What is the probability that someone chosen at random is left-handed and does not wear glasses? (State carefully any assumptions you make.)

3 A bag contains 20 counters, of which 4 are red, 7 are blue and 9 are black. What is the probability that a counter picked at random is either red or blue?

4 Indira passes through a set of traffic lights and a level crossing when she goes to work. The probability that the lights are red when she gets to them is $\frac{3}{8}$ and the probability that the crossing is closed is $\frac{2}{15}$. She is late for work if she has to stop for both. What is the probability that she is late for work? (State carefully any assumptions you make.)

6.4 Tree diagrams

In tasksheet 3 you looked at the different choices made by customers at a restaurant. The analysis of this type of problem is often clearer if you use a **tree diagram**.

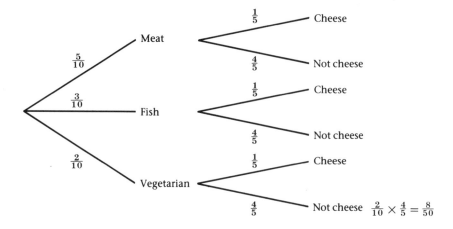

The six different combinations are represented by the six branches of the tree diagram.

The probability of each sequence of events (the branch probability) is calculated by multiplying the probabilities along the branches.

(a) Why do you multiply the probabilities in this case?

(b) Calculate the six branch probabilities.

(c) Add up these six probabilities and explain why the total must equal 1.

TASKSHEET 4 — Tree diagrams (page 73)

> The probability that a particular sequence of events will take place is found by multiplying the probabilities along the corresponding sequence of branches.
>
> The branches on a tree diagram represent mutually exclusive sequences of events so the probability that one or other of several particular sequences will take place can be found by adding their individual probabilities.

EXAMPLE 2

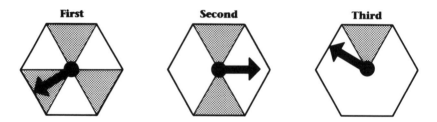

A tombola game at a village fête uses three hexagonal spinners which you spin in the order shown. Each spinner is painted blue and white as shown. Draw a tree diagram to show the possible outcomes for the **first two spins** and use it to calculate the probability of scoring at least one blue after two spins.

SOLUTION

Assume that the spinners are independent.

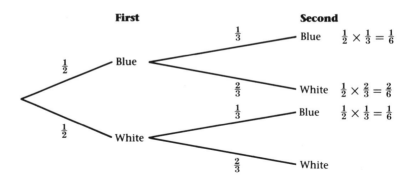

The probability of at least one blue on the first two spins is:

$$\tfrac{1}{6} + \tfrac{2}{6} + \tfrac{1}{6} = \tfrac{4}{6} = \tfrac{2}{3}$$

You win a prize if you score blue on each of the three spinners. If you score blue on the first two spinners but fail on the third then you get another go.

Copy and extend the tree diagram to include the third spinner. Hence calculate:

(a) the probability that you win a prize;

(b) the probability that you get a second go.

After working through this chapter you should:

1 understand the concept of a probability based on:

- mathematical ideas of symmetry,
- relative frequency obtained from experimental evidence;

2 know the terms:

- mutually exclusive events,
- independent events;

3 know when to **add** and when to **multiply** probabilities;

4 know how to construct and use a tree diagram.

Investigating probability

1 Toss a coin 5 times and make a note of how many heads you get. If you toss a coin 5 times and get 4 heads, do you still think that the probability of a tail is equal to that of a head? (Justify your answer.)

A probability such as '1 in 2' can be written as:

● a fraction, $\frac{1}{2}$;

● a decimal, 0·5;

● a percentage, 50%.

Note that 50% is the same as 50 in 100 or 0·5 or $\frac{1}{2}$.

---

2 Write the probability '1 in 4' as:

(a) a fraction;

(b) a decimal;

(c) a percentage.

3 In the game of Ludo you throw a die before you move and you must throw a six to start. Explain why the probability of throwing a six is $\frac{1}{6}$ if the die is fair.

4 A spinner like the one illustrated is used in a game. Calculate the probability that the spinner stops in a shaded triangle. (Express your answer as a decimal.)

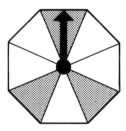

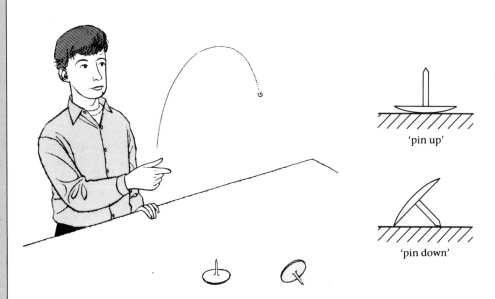

If you toss a drawing pin it can land 'pin up' or 'pin down'. However, there is no reason to suppose that these two outcomes are equally likely and so you cannot assume that the probability of it landing 'pin up' is $\frac{1}{2}$. You have to base your estimate of the probability on past experience or experimental evidence.

5   (a) Toss a drawing pin 10 times and note how many times it lands 'pin up'. Write down the probability of the drawing pin landing 'pin up' based on this evidence. Write your answer as a percentage.

    (b) Now toss the pin a further 40 times and again note how many times it lands 'pin up'. (You have now tossed it 50 times.) Write down a probability for the pin landing 'pin up' based on this increased evidence (i.e. 50 throws). Write your answer as a percentage.

    (c) Which of your answers, (a) or (b), do you think is a more accurate estimate of the actual probability that the drawing pin lands 'pin up'.

    (d) How many times do you have to toss a drawing pin before you predict accurately the probability of it landing 'pin up'?

Adding probabilities

For this tasksheet, you may find it helpful to have a standard pack of 52 playing cards to look at.

If you pick a card at random, then the outcome can be described in several ways. These are called **events**. Consider the following possible events:

- A – the card is a spade;
- B – the card is an ace;
- C – the card is the king of clubs;
- D – the card is from a red suit.

1 Which pairs of events are mutually exclusive?

2 The probability that event A occurs when you pick a card is denoted by P(A).

(a) What do you think P(B) denotes?

(b) Write down as a fraction with denominator 52:

(i) P(A)   (ii) P(B)   (iii) P(C)   (iv) P(D)

3 Events A and D are mutually exclusive.

(a) From a pack of cards, take out all those cards which can be described by **either** A **or** D and note how many there are.

(b) Write down P(A or D).

(c) What simple relationship is there between P(A), P(D) and P(A or D)?

4 Repeat question 3 for a different pair of mutually exclusive events.

5 Find P(A or B) and explain why the relationship you discovered for mutually exclusive events does not apply to events which are **not** mutually exclusive. (Note that P(A or B) means the probability that a card is either in A or B or in both.)

Multiplying probabilities

In a restaurant, customers order for their main course meat (event M), fish (event F) or a vegetarian meal (event V). The waiter estimates from experience that 50% of customers order meat, 30% order fish and the remaining 20% order a vegetarian meal. Following their main meal, some customers (20%) order cheese and biscuits (event C).

The two-way table shows this information.

	Cheese (C)	Not cheese (not C)	Total
Meat (M)	10	40	50
Fish (F)	6	24	30
Vegetarian (V)	4	16	20
Total	20	80	100

1 Explain why the events M, F and V are mutually exclusive.

2 Write as a decimal:

(a) P(M)   (b) P(F)   (c) P(V)   (d) P(C)   (e) P(not C)

3 (a) Of the thirty customers who ordered fish, only six then have cheese. What is the probability that a particular customer who has had fish will follow this with cheese?

(b) What is the probability that a customer orders cheese if you know that she has previously ordered a vegetarian meal?

(c) What is the probability that a customer orders cheese if you know he has previously ordered meat?

You have seen that the probability that a customer orders cheese is unaffected by what they have previously ordered for the main course. This means that 'meat and cheese', 'fish and cheese', and 'vegetarian and cheese' are all pairs of **independent events**.

4 Six customers out of every hundred order fish and cheese. So P(F and C) = 0·06.

What simple relationship exists between P(F), P(C) and P(F and C)?

5 (a) What simple relationship exists between P(*M*), P(*C*) and P(*M* and *C*)?

(b) What simple relationship exists between P(*V*), P(*C*) and P(*V* and *C*)?

It is important to remember that the results established here apply to pairs of **independent** events. (Two events are independent if the occurrence of one event does not affect the probability of the other occurring.)

6 Not all pairs of events are independent. Consider the following events:

- *A* – I walk to work today.

- *B* – It rains today.

Explain why it is unlikely that these events are independent.

Tree diagrams

Suppose you have two bags, one with 1 red counter and 2 white counters, the other with 3 red counters and 1 blue counter. (You may find it helpful to make up two bags or envelopes like this.) You pick one counter at random from each bag.

1 Copy and complete the tree diagram.

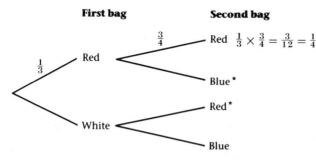

First bag

Second bag

$\frac{3}{4}$ — Red $\frac{1}{3} \times \frac{3}{4} = \frac{3}{12} = \frac{1}{4}$

$\frac{1}{3}$ Red

Blue*

Red*

White

Blue

There are four possible outcomes, each represented by a branch. These outcomes are mutually exclusive.

2 Explain why the four branch probabilities must add up to 1.

To obtain the probability that you pick exactly one red counter, you should **add** the branch probabilities which have just one red in the sequence of events. These are marked with a star on the tree diagram.

3 (a) Explain why you can add these probabilities, and calculate the probability that you pick exactly one red counter.

4 What is the probability that you pick:

(a) two different-coloured counters; (b) two counters with the same colour?

The diagram below shows all the possible outcomes for the problem of picking two counters, one from each bag. Each individual counter is listed because each has the same probability of being picked – the possible outcomes are **equally likely**.

	First bag		
	R	W	W
R	•	⊙	⊙
R	•	⊙	⊙
R	•	⊙	⊙
B	⊙	•	•

Second bag

The dots with rings around are the outcomes with just one red counter.

This shows that the probability of picking just one red is $\frac{7}{12}$.

5 Check that this agrees with the result you found using a tree diagram.

Solutions

1 The survey

1.1 Samples and censuses

About 100000 16-year-olds left school for youth training in 1990.

(a) Use the histogram to estimate the total number of 16-year-olds staying on in education in 1990.

(b) Estimate the number of 16-year-olds in the other categories.

(c) Use your answers to (a) and (b) to estimate how many 16-year-olds there were in total in 1990.

(d) Calculate percentages and draw a pie chart for 1990 similar to the one shown for 1991.

(e) Is the conclusion of the newspaper headline justified?

(a) Approximately 300000 stayed in education.

(b) The numbers of 16-year-olds in the other categories are:

Youth training	100000
Employment	100000
Not any	40000
Not known	30000

(c) The total was 570000.

(d) The percentages are as follows:

Education	$300000 \div 570000 \approx 0 \cdot 53 = 53\%$
Youth training	$100000 \div 570000 \approx 0 \cdot 18 = 18\%$
Employment	$100000 \div 570000 \approx 0 \cdot 18 = 18\%$
Not any	$40000 \div 570000 \approx 0 \cdot 07 = 7\%$
Not known	$30000 \div 570000 \approx 0 \cdot 05 = 5\%$
	$\overline{101\%}$

The total should be 100% but the figures have been rounded, which accounts for the discrepancy. You can construct a pie chart using either a pie chart scale marked in percentages or a protractor. If you use a protractor, remember that each percentage point is $3 \cdot 6°$ on the scale so 53% would need a $53 \times 3 \cdot 6° = 191°$ sector.

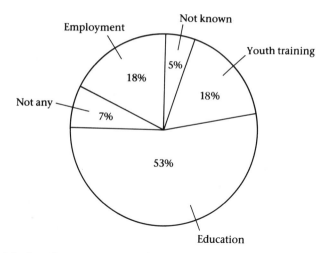

(e) The headline is justified. 61% is significantly higher than 53%.

1.2 Pose the question

Criticise the following questions and in each case suggest a way of improving them.

(a) How big are you?

(b) What do you think of the present government?

(c) How much do you spend on clothes?   Less than average ☐
                                          About average ☐
                                          More than average ☐

(d) What do you think of the new improved canteen menu?

(a) It is unclear what 'big' means. It could, for example, refer to either height or weight. It should be replaced by a more specific question. Take care that the question is not offensive!

(b) The question is unclear. What sort of response is expected? Would a single word or phrase such as 'not a lot' suffice? It is also unreasonable if you are expected to write several pages in response. Replace it with a question where the expected response is well defined. You could, for example, ask people to tick boxes or limit the response to fewer than twenty words.

(c) It is unclear what 'average' means in this question. Replace 'average' with a specific amount such as £10 per week.

(d) This is a leading question. The word 'improved' suggests that the person answering the question ought to think that the menu is better. As in part (b), it would be better to ask a question which expects a well-defined response.

1.3   Collect the data

> Why might there be bias in the method used for picking the sample in each of the following?
>
> (a) A secondary school is holding its own mock election just before a general election. A pupil asks the other pupils in the class how they intend to vote. This is then used to predict the result for the school.
>
> (b) A student is doing a survey into students' attitudes to the college canteen. She picks students at random from the dinner queue as her sample.

(a) The sample would be biased. The best you can hope for is that the class is representative of a particular age group. If it is a class of 16-year-olds, they would not necessarily represent the views of 12-year-olds!

(b) The sample would be biased because the students in the queue are likely to have a reasonably positive attitude or they would not be using the canteen in the first place!

2 Displaying frequency

2.2   Frequency graphs

> (a) Display these results on a bar graph.
>
> (b) Why might McTavish's want this information?

(a) You could draw the graph with the bars representing the numbers of females and males who prefer each burger drawn end-to-end to stress the total number of people who prefer each burger.

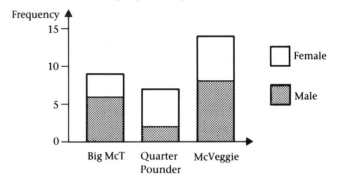

Alternatively, it could be drawn with the bars side-by-side if you want to show the differences between the numbers of females and males who prefer each burger.

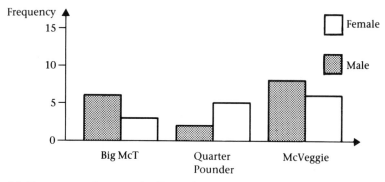

(b) To manage their stock efficiently, McTavish's need to assess demand. They might also need to assess where they should be putting their marketing effort.

Suppose the intervals are 0–, 15– and 30–45.

(a) Produce a tally and draw the frequency graph.

(b) Do you think this choice of interval is better or worse than the one used in the example? Explain.

(a)

Time spent (minutes)	0–	15–	30–45
Tally	ЖТ IIII	ЖТ ЖТ III	ЖТ III
Frequency	9	13	8

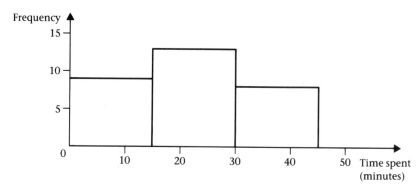

(b) This choice of interval is probably not as good as the one in the example. The information it provides about how the values are distributed is not as detailed.

77

EXERCISE 1

1

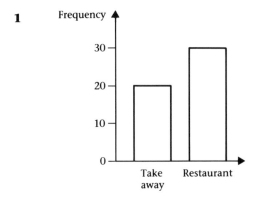

2 (a)

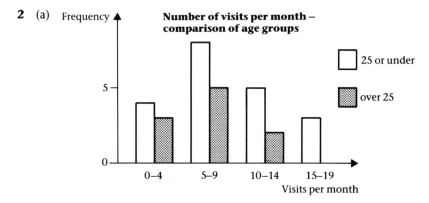

(b) It is probably better to draw the bars side-by-side to show the comparison between the two age groups. This comparison could be interesting. If the bars are drawn end-to-end the graph would show the combined totals for both age groups.

(c) The most common number of visits per month is between 5 and 9.

(d) It is not very easy to compare the number of visits for each age group because there were more people in the '25 and under' category. You could say that older people in this sample appear to make a smaller number of visits than younger people.

2.3   Choosing intervals

> Neither of the previous groupings is ideal. What grouping would you recommend the market researchers to use and why?

The market researchers should choose a grouping which is between 1 and 10 as you have seen that 1 gives too much detail and 10 does not give enough. A grouping of 3 or 4 might be sensible.

EXERCISE 2

1 (a)

Amount taken (£)	400–	500–	600–	700–	800–	900–	1000–	1100
Tally	JHT	JHT				II		II

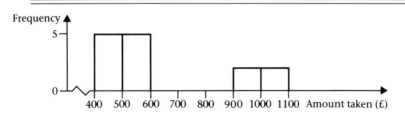

(b) The graph has two peaks – one at about £500 and one at about £1000. A possible explanation is that there is a big difference between the weekday and the weekend takings.

2 (a)

Volume (ml)		470–	480–	490–	500–	510–520
Tally		I	IIII	JHT I	IIII	I

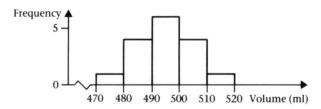

(b) The volume produced by the dispenser needs to be increased, since most of the McThick Shakes sold at the moment will be under 500 ml. It should be adjusted so that each shake gets about 10–15 ml more. McTavish's should probably consider getting an engineer to mend their dispenser to give more even quantities!

2.4 Frequency polygons

Draw the frequency polygon for Saturday.

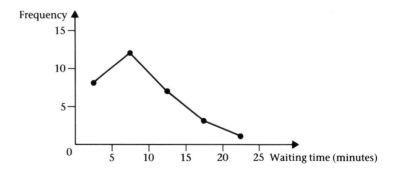

> (a) Describe the main difference between the two distributions.
>
> (b) Why might you have expected such a difference?
>
> (c) What recommendation would you make to the manager of McTavish's on the basis of this evidence?

(a) The frequency distribution for Saturday is more spread out and the peak waiting time is greater.

(b) It is likely that Saturday is busier than Monday and so people have to wait longer to be served.

(c) Perhaps she should consider employing more staff on Saturdays.

EXERCISE 4

1 (a)

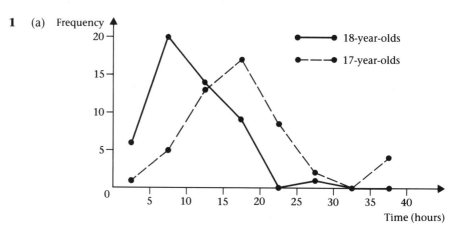

(b) The graph shows that the 18-year-olds watched much less television than the 17-year-olds. This could be because the third week in May is a time when most 18-year-olds are busy revising for public exams. Many of the 17-year-olds may have been on two-year courses and would therefore not have had such important exams during the summer.

3 Correlation

3.1 Two-way tables

> (a) How many boys opted for games?
>
> (b) How many students altogether did **not** opt for games?
>
> (c) 'More girls than boys opt for games so a girl is more likely to do games than a boy.' Do you agree with this conclusion?
>
> (d) What conclusions (if any) can you draw?

(a) The number of boys who opted for games can be found by subtracting the number of boys who did not opt for games (10) from the total number of boys (50).

Number of boys who opted for games = 50 − 10 = 40

(b) You know that the number of students who opted for games was 40 + 49 = 89. The total number of students was 120 so the number of students who did not opt for games was 120 − 89 = 31.

(c) 49 girls opted for games compared to 40 boys so the first part of the statement is true. The total number of girls is 120 − 50 = 70 compared to 50 boys.
If you use percentages, $\frac{49}{70}$ = 70% of girls opt for games compared with $\frac{40}{50}$ = 80% of boys. This shows that the conclusion is not true.

(d) The complete table is as follows.

	Games	Other	Total
Boys	40	10	50
Girls	49	21	70
Total	89	31	120

From the table you can see that:

- there are 20 more girls than boys in the sixth form;

- about three times as many students opt for games as for other activities.

From part (c) you know that a boy is more likely to opt for games than a girl.

EXERCISE 1

1

	Male	Female	Total
Like	90	10	100
Dislike	10	20	30
No opinion	40	30	70
Total	140	60	200

2 (a) You are told that 103 students opted for word processing only, so 103 must go in cell *b*. You are also told that students must study word processing or databases or both, so 0 should go in cell *c*.

(b)

	WP	Not WP	Total
DB	47	9	56
Not DB	103	0	103
Total	150	9	159

(c) From the table you can see that 56 students studied databases.

3 (a)

	Conservative	Labour	Liberal Democrat	Total
Male	232	179	83	494
Female	217	148	141	506
Total	449	327	224	1000

(b) $\frac{83}{224} \approx 37\%$ of Liberal Democrat voters are male.

(c) $\frac{83}{494} \approx 17\%$ of males intend to vote Liberal Democrat.

4 (a)

	Method X	Method Y	Total
Germinated	12	13	25
Failed to germinate	13	17	30
Total	25	30	55

(b) For method X, $\frac{12}{25} = 48\%$ germinate. For method Y, $\frac{13}{30} \approx 43\%$ germinate. These results suggest that method X is more effective for growing beans.

5 (a)

	To and from work	Other reasons for travel	Total
Car	14	58	72
Train	3	4	7
Bus	2	4	6
Other	7	8	15
Total	26	74	100

(b) $\frac{3}{7} \approx 43\%$ of the distance travelled by train was for the purpose of going to and from work.

(c) $\frac{3}{26} \approx 12\%$ of the distance travelled going to and from work was travelled by train.

6 The information given can be displayed in a table. The complete table is as follows.

	Men	Women	Total
Under 30	20	35	55
30 or over	20	25	45
Total	40	60	100

From the table you can see that 60% of the workers are women.

3.2 Scatter graphs

> What similarities and what differences between the two situations are illustrated by the graphs? Give possible reasons for these similarities and differences.

The trend is the same on both graphs – as the diameter increases so does the circumference.
The data for the circular objects lie on a straight line whereas the data for people's heads do not.
Circular objects such as CDs follow the rule $C = \pi d$. The circumference is directly proportional to the diameter so a graph of circumference against diameter will be a straight line through the origin with gradient π. There is no such rule for heads but because their circumferences are very roughly circular in shape you would expect a similar relationship.

> Draw a sketch of a scatter graph which shows the type of graph you would expect if you plotted:
>
> (a) height against weight;
>
> (b) arm length against leg length;
>
> (c) head diameter against age for adults.

(a)

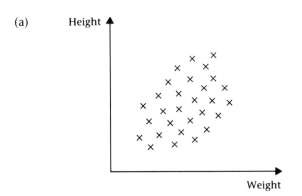

(b)   Arm length

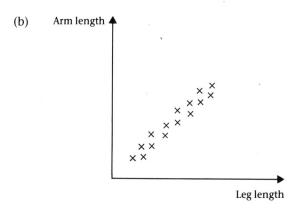

Leg length

(c)   Head diameter

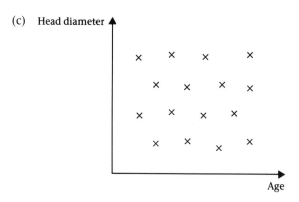

Age

Does this prove that storks bring babies?

There is no logical reason why the number of storks should be connected to the number of babies born. A correlation does not prove that a relationship exists.

3.3   Making predictions

(a) What widths would you recommend for small and large helmets?

(b) Describe the method you used to find these widths.

(a) The small helmet should have a width of 14·2 cm and the large helmet should have a width of 16·0 cm.

(b) One method is as follows. A 'best straight line' is fitted by eye through the scattered points. It is made to pass through the mean. It represents the assumed connection between width and length. The widths corresponding to the lengths 17·3 cm and 20·3 cm can be read off the line.

You may have slightly different answers to part (a) because you fitted a different 'best straight line'.

EXERCISE 2

1 (a) It would be reasonable to expect people with long arms to have long fingers.

(b) Mean finger length $= \dfrac{46 \cdot 8}{7} = 6 \cdot 7 \, \text{cm}$ (to 1 d.p.)

Mean arm length $= \dfrac{441 \cdot 5}{7} = 63 \cdot 1 \, \text{cm}$ (to 1 d.p.)

(c)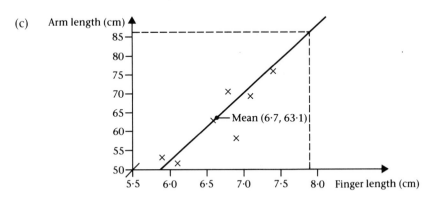

(d) The correlation between arm length and finger length is high.

(e) The estimate of the arm length of a person whose finger length is known to be 7·9 cm is 86 cm. It is found as shown on the graph in (c).

2

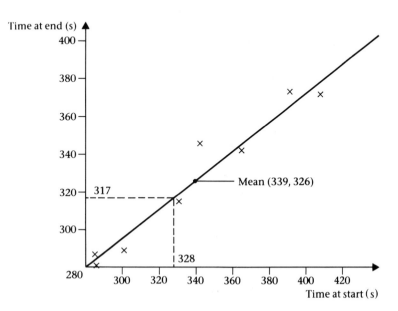

The estimated time at the end of the week for the girl who left early is 317 seconds.

85

3 (a)

The line of best fit and the mean value (7·2, 7·8) ignore the data from Northern Ireland (see part (c)).

(b) An estimate for the crime rate in a region where unemployment is 14% is 13·5%.

(c) The graph suggests that in Northern Ireland there is a different relationship between crime and unemployment from that in the rest of the United Kingdom.

4 An average value

4.1 What is average?

EXERCISE 1

1 The mean is $\dfrac{5 + 5 + 10 + 25 + 5 + 8 + 7 + 10 + 15}{9}$ = £10.

The amounts arranged in order are £5, £5, £5, £7, £8, £10, £10, £15, £25. The median is £8. The mode is £5.

2 (a) The mean is $\dfrac{28 + 30 + 30 + 32 + 34 + 36 + 38 + 38 + 38 + 40}{10}$ = 34·4 inches.

The median is $\dfrac{34 + 36}{2}$ = 35 inches.

The mode of the sizes is 38.

(b) The mode is the most popular size so the shopkeeper should make sure that there are plenty of T-shirts of this size in stock.

3   The shopkeeper is using the mean. The number of shoes sold will vary from week to week and different types of shoe will make different profits. The mean takes all this variation into account in the figure for the total profit per week.

4   (a) The total number of home 'goals for' is 678.
The total number of away 'goals for' is 496.

$$\text{The mean number of 'goals for' is } \frac{678 + 496}{22} = \frac{1174}{22} = 53{\cdot}4.$$

This is 1·3 goals per match.

(b) The total number of home 'goals against' is 496.
The total number of away 'goals against' is 678.

$$\text{The mean number of 'goals against' is } \frac{496 + 678}{22} = \frac{1174}{22} = 53{\cdot}4.$$

(c) The answers to (a) and (b) have to be the same because every goal scored for one team is a goal against another team.

5E   The total number of trainees is $17 + 21 + 18 + 22 + 19 + 23 = 120$.
The total estimated time is:

$(17 \times 53) + (21 \times 62) + (18 \times 58) + (22 \times 52) + (19 \times 61) + (23 \times 55)$
$= 6815$ seconds

The mean estimate for all trainees is $\frac{6815}{120} = 56{\cdot}8$ seconds (to 1 d.p.).

4.2   Dealing with repetition

Use this method to calculate the mean.

52 goals were scored by the home teams and 29 were scored by the away teams. The total number of goals scored was $52 + 29 = 81$.
The mean number of goals scored is $\frac{81}{64} = 1{\cdot}3$ (to 1 d.p.).

(a) Use the frequency table to explain why the total number of goals is:

$(0 \times 22) + (1 \times 21) + (2 \times 11) + (3 \times 4) + (4 \times 4) + (5 \times 2)$

(b) Explain how you can use the frequency table to calculate the total number of teams taking part.

(c) Calculate the mean number of goals per team.

(d) Explain how you can use the frequency table to calculate the median number of goals scored.

(a) You can see from the frequency table that 22 teams did not score, 21 teams scored one goal, 11 teams scored two goals, 4 teams scored three goals, 4 teams scored four goals and 2 teams scored five goals. The total number of goals scored is:

$$(0 \times 22) + (1 \times 21) + (2 \times 11) + (3 \times 4) + (4 \times 4) + (5 \times 2)$$

(b) The number of teams that took part is given by the total of the frequency column:

$$22 + 21 + 11 + 4 + 4 + 2 = 64$$

(c) From (a) the total number of goals scored is $21 + 22 + 12 + 16 + 10 = 81$. The mean number of goals scored is $\frac{81}{64} = 1.3$ (to 1 d.p.).

(d) 64 teams took part, so the median number of goals scored is the average of the number of goals scored by the 32nd and 33rd teams. The frequency table shows that 22 teams did not score and 43 teams scored one goal. Both the 32nd and 33rd teams must have scored one goal, so the median number of goals scored is 1.

EXERCISE 2

1 (a) The number of students who took part in the survey was:

$$5 + 8 + 25 + 49 + 51 + 37 + 17 + 8 = 200$$

(b) The number of meals which included chips was:

$$(0 \times 5) + (1 \times 8) + (2 \times 25) + (3 \times 49) + (4 \times 51) + (5 \times 37) + (6 \times 17) + (7 \times 8)$$
$$= 752$$

The mean number of times per week that a student had chips with a meal was $\frac{752}{200} = 3.76$ or about 4 times a week.

4.3   Grouped data

(a) Why is this a reasonable estimate?

(b) About how long did the eight customers who each waited between 5 and 10 minutes spend waiting in total?

(c) Use this method to calculate a reasonable estimate of the total time spent waiting by all the customers in the survey.

(d) How many customers were involved in the survey?

(e) Use your answers to (c) and (d) to calculate an estimate of the mean time customers spent waiting to be served.

(a) The number of customers who took less than 17·5 minutes is likely to be the same as the number of customers who took more than 17·5 minutes. 17·5 minutes is therefore a reasonable estimate of an average value for the four customers.

(b) The total waiting time for the customers who waited between 5 and 10 minutes was $8 \times 7·5 = 60$ minutes.

(c) An estimate of the total waiting time for all the customers in the survey is:

$$(13 \times 2·5) + (8 \times 7·5) + (5 \times 12·5) + (4 \times 17·5) = 225 \text{ minutes}$$

(d) The number of customers involved in the survey was
$13 + 8 + 5 + 4 = 30$.

(e) The mean waiting time was $\frac{225}{30} = 7·5$ minutes.

> A student tried to answer the question above by saying that as there are four data items (55, 65, 75 and 85) the mean should be $6800 \div 4 = 1700 \, \text{kg}$. Why is this obviously wrong?

The mean has to lie somewhere in the range 50 to 90 kg and is likely to be near the middle, around 70 kg. 1700 kg is therefore obviously wrong.

EXERCISE 3

Note: All the means calculated in this exercise are **estimates**.

1 (a) The number of students who took part in the race was:

$$1 + 5 + 23 + 47 + 13 + 1 = 90$$

(b) The total time for completing the course was:

$$(1 \times 45) + (5 \times 55) + (23 \times 65) + (47 \times 75) + (13 \times 85) + (1 \times 95)$$
$$= 6540 \text{ seconds}$$

The mean time for completing the course is $\frac{6540}{90} = 72·7$ seconds (to 1 d.p.).

2 (a) Kim kept a record for $2 + 6 + 18 + 4 + 0 = 30$ days.

(b) The total time for the journey was:

$$(2 \times 22·5) + (6 \times 27·5) + (18 \times 32·5) + (4 \times 37·5) + (0 \times 42·5)$$
$$= 945 \text{ minutes}$$

The mean time for the journey was $\frac{945}{30} = 31·5$ minutes.

3 (a) Mukul kept a record for $25 + 12 + 7 + 15 + 2 + 0 + 5 + 1 = 67$ days.
The total rainfall was:

$$(25 \times 2) + (12 \times 6) + (7 \times 10) + (15 \times 14) + (2 \times 18) + (0 \times 22) +$$
$$(5 \times 26) + (1 \times 30)$$
$$= 598 \text{ mm}$$

The mean rainfall per day was $\frac{598}{67} = 8·9$ mm (to 1 d.p.).

(b) An estimate of the annual rainfall is $8 \cdot 9 \times 365 = 3248 \cdot 5$ mm. This is about 325 cm.

(c) This estimate would be high for most places in Britain, where rainfall varies from month to month. Perhaps Mukul chose the wettest time of the year.

5 Measures of spread

5.1 Cumulative frequency

> (a) How many runners completed the course in under $1\frac{1}{2}$ hours?
>
> (b) Estimate the time taken by the median runner (the runner who finished 179th).

(a) $1\frac{1}{2}$ hours is 90 minutes. The number of runners who completed the race in under $1\frac{1}{2}$ hours was $2 + 14 + 31 = 47$.

(b) 106 runners took less than 100 minutes and 214 runners took less than 110 minutes. The 179th runner took about 107 minutes.

> (a) 25% of the students gained a grade A. What is the minimum mark needed for an A grade?
>
> (b) 25% of students failed the exam. What was the pass mark?

(a) 25% of 188 is $0 \cdot 25 \times 188 = 47$.
$188 - 47 = 141$
From the graph, at a cumulative frequency of 141 the mark is 78. The minimum mark needed for an A grade is 78.

(b) From the graph, at a cumulative frequency of 47 the mark is 59. The pass mark is 59.

5.2 Quartiles

EXERCISE 1

1 In rank order the scores are 1, 4, 9, 11, 13, 18, 21, 31, 32, 52 and 56.
The median is the sixth data item, which is 18.
The upper quartile is the ninth data item, which is 32.
The lower quartile is the third data item, which is 9.

2 In rank order the data are 1, 2, 2, 2, 2, 3, 3, 3, 4 and 5.

The median is the average of the fifth and sixth data items, $\dfrac{2 + 3}{2} = 2 \cdot 5$.

The upper quartile is the eighth data item, which is 3.
The lower quartile is the third data item, which is 2.

3 (a)

Income (£000s)	4	8	12	16	20	24	28	32
Cumulative frequency	5	29	74	130	167	186	197	200

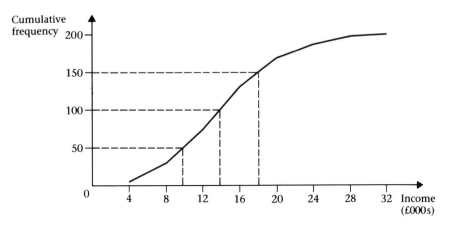

(b) The median is £14000.
The upper quartile is £18000.
The lower quartile is £10000.
(All the values are to the nearest £500.)

5.3 Spread

> For each of the data sets A, B and C:
>
> (a) calculate the mean;   (b) find the median.
>
> What do you notice about these statistics?

(a)

Data set	Mean
A	$\dfrac{108{\cdot}6}{30} = 3{\cdot}62$
B	$\dfrac{108{\cdot}0}{30} = 3{\cdot}60$
C	$\dfrac{107{\cdot}8}{30} \approx 3{\cdot}59$

(b)

Data set	Median
A	3·5
B	3·5
C	3·5

The medians of the three data sets are identical. The means are almost equal. The means are very close to the medians.

> (a) Use the frequency polygons to describe how the spreads of the three data sets differ.
>
> (b) Suggest a statistic to measure the spread of data sets such as those shown.

(a) Data set B has the widest spread. The range of the data is from 1·2 kg to 5·6 kg.

Data set C has the narrowest spread. The range of the data is from 2·4 kg to 4·8 kg. It also has the most pronounced peak at around the mean value of 3·6 kg.

Data set B has the least pronounced peak and the greatest spread.

Data set A is like C in shape but more widely spread than C.

(b) You may have chosen the range. This is often used. The interquartile range, which gives the range between the upper and lower quartiles, could also be used because it represents the spread of the middle 50% of the data.

> Calculate estimates of the range and interquartile range for the fell race data.

The range is about $140 - 60 = 80$ minutes.

The interquartile range is the difference in times of the 89th and 268th runner, which is $116 - 97 = 19$ minutes.

5.4 Box and whisker diagrams

> (a) Which parts of the data form the box?
>
> (b) Which parts of the data form the whiskers?
>
> (c) How is the range shown?
>
> (d) How is the interquartile range shown?

(a) The box is formed by the data between the upper and lower quartile, which is the middle 50% of the data. The line through the box marks the median value.

(b) The left-hand whisker is formed by the data between the lowest data item and the lower quartile. The right-hand whisker is formed by the data between the upper quartile and the highest value.

(c) The range is represented by the distance between the two markers at the extreme ends of the whiskers.

(d) The interquartile range is represented by the length of the box.

> Draw box and whisker diagrams for the questions in Exercise 1.

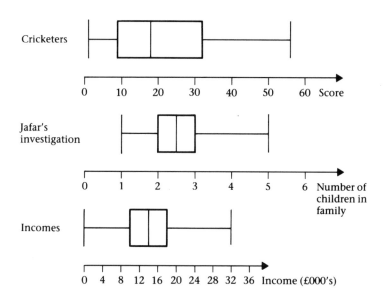

6 Probability

6.1   Types of probability

> Copy the probability line and mark on the probability of:
>
> (a) getting a six when you throw a die;
>
> (b) **not** getting a six when you throw a die;
>
> (c) getting a spade when you pick a card from a well-shuffled pack;
>
> (d) an American tennis player winning the women's championship at Wimbledon next year. Justify your answer.

The probabilities are:

(a) $\frac{1}{6}$　(b) $\frac{5}{6}$　(c) $\frac{1}{4}$

(d) There are many possibilities. For example, the probability could depend on:

- how many American women enter the competition;
- whether there is a very good American player;
- how many very good players there are from elsewhere in the world.

6.2　Adding probabilities

> Which card fits both the event 'the card is a club' and the event 'the card is an ace'?

The ace of clubs is both an ace and a club.

> In example 1, find:
>
> (a) P(not B);　(b) P(A or C);　(c) P(A or B or C);
>
> (d) P(B or not B).

(a) P(not B) = 1 − P(B) = 1 − 0·3 = 0·7

(b) P(A or C) = P(A) + P(C) = 0·5 + 0·2 = 0·7

(c) P(A or B or C) = P(A) + P(B) + P(C) = 0·5 + 0·3 + 0·2 = 1
P(A or B or C) = 1 can be written down immediately because A, B and C are mutually exclusive and exhaustive.

(d) P(B or not B) = P(B) + P(not B) = 0·3 + 0·7 = 1
P(B or not B) = 1 can be written down immediately because event B and event not B are mutually exclusive and exhaustive – one or the other must happen but they cannot both happen.

6.3　Multiplying probabilities

> (a) Would it be reasonable to assume that the two events 'Mary wins a prize in the raffle' and 'Mary's car breaks down' are independent?
>
> (b) Are these events mutually exclusive?

(a) It is reasonable to assume that the two events are independent because winning a raffle should not affect Mary's car.

(b) The events are not mutually exclusive because it is possible that she wins a raffle and her car breaks down.

What assumption has been made in the solution above?

It has been assumed that the colour of a bicycle is independent of whether or not it has faulty brakes.

EXERCISE 1

1 For the first bag, P(red) = $\frac{3}{8}$
For the second bag, P(red) = $\frac{5}{12}$
P(both red) = $\frac{3}{8} \times \frac{5}{12} = \frac{15}{96} = \frac{5}{32}$

2 P(left-handed) = $\frac{2}{9}$
P(does not wear glasses) = $1 - \frac{3}{10} = \frac{7}{10}$
P(left-handed and does not wear glasses) = $\frac{2}{9} \times \frac{7}{10} = \frac{14}{90} = \frac{7}{45}$
The calculation assumes that the wearing of glasses is independent of being left- or right-handed.

3 P(red or blue) = $\frac{4}{20} + \frac{7}{20} = \frac{11}{20}$

4 P(she is late for work) = P(the lights are red and the crossing is closed)
$= \frac{3}{8} \times \frac{2}{15} = \frac{6}{120} = \frac{1}{20}$
The calculation assumes that the lights and the level crossing operate independently.

6.4 Tree diagrams

(a) Why do you multiply the probabilities in this case?

(b) Calculate the six branch probabilities.

(c) Add up these six probabilities and explain why the total must equal 1.

(a) You multiply probabilities in this case because the events are independent. Whether or not customers order cheese does not depend on what they had for their main meals.

(b) P(meat and cheese) $= \frac{5}{10} \times \frac{1}{5} = \frac{5}{50}$
P(meat and not cheese) $= \frac{5}{10} \times \frac{4}{5} = \frac{20}{50}$
P(fish and cheese) $= \frac{3}{10} \times \frac{1}{5} = \frac{3}{50}$
P(fish and not cheese) $= \frac{3}{10} \times \frac{4}{5} = \frac{12}{50}$
P(vegetarian and cheese) $= \frac{2}{10} \times \frac{1}{5} = \frac{2}{50}$
P(vegetarian and not cheese) $= \frac{2}{10} \times \frac{4}{5} = \frac{8}{50}$

(c) $\dfrac{5 + 20 + 3 + 12 + 2 + 8}{50} = \dfrac{50}{50} = 1$

The total must be 1 because the six events of the branch probabilities are mutually exclusive and exhaustive – no two can happen at the same time but one of them must happen.

> Copy and extend the tree diagram to include the third spinner. Hence calculate:
>
> (a) the probability that you win a prize,
>
> (b) the probability that you get a second go.

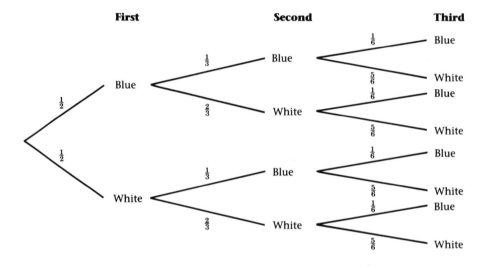

(a) To win a prize you need blue on each of the three spinners.
$P(\text{win a prize}) = \frac{1}{2} \times \frac{1}{3} \times \frac{1}{6} = \frac{1}{36}$

(b) To get a second go you need blue on the first and second spinners and white on the third.
$P(\text{get a second go}) = \frac{1}{2} \times \frac{1}{3} \times \frac{5}{6} = \frac{5}{36}$